All About Bulbs

Writers

Alvin Horton
James McNair

Project Editor

Michael D. Smith

Illustrators

Ron Hildebrand
Cyndie Clark-Huegel

2 Acknowledgments

Ortho Books

Publisher
Robert L. Iacopi

Editorial Supervisor
Robert J. Dolezal

Production Director
Ernie S. Tasaki

Managing Editors
Anne Coolman
Mike Smith
Sally Smith

System Manager
Leonard D. Grotta

National Sales Manager
Charles H. Aydelotte

Marketing Specialist
Susan B. Boyle

Operations Assistant
Georgiann Wright

Senior Technical Analyst
J. A. Crozier, Jr.

Chevron Chemical Company
575 Market Street, San Francisco, CA 94105

Front cover: A mixed border of bulbs and shrubs. The daffodils in the background are *Narcissus tazetta*; the tulips in the foreground are mixed colors of *Tulipa kaufmaniana*.

Back cover: Flower arrangements can be made of potted plants as well as of cut flowers. From top to bottom, these are daffodil 'King Alfred', tulip 'Plaisir', hyacinth 'L'Innocence', and grape hyacinth.

Title page: Crocus foretells the brightness and sunshine of spring. These are 'Pickwick' and 'Yellow'.

Consultants
Dr. August De Hertogh
North Carolina State University

Stan Farwig
Concord, California

Vic Girard
Concord, California

Wayne Roderick
Orinda, California

Composition and Pagination
Linda M. Bouchard
William F. Yusavage

Copyeditors
Melinda Levine
Loralee Windsor

Design Consultant
Christine Brundage

Indexer
Frances Bowles

Proofreaders
Melinda Levine
Kate Rider
Suzanne Sherman

Photo Editor
Pamela Peirce

Production Artists
Deborah Cowder
Lezlly Freier
Anne Pederson

Adaptation Map Editors
Charmain Giuliani
San Francisco, California

Esta Kornfield
San Francisco, California

Photographs

William C. Aplin
Page 46R

James A. Bauml
Pages 48R, 78R, 82R

Clyde Childress
Page 19

C. Gerald Clear
(Helen Crocker Russell Library)
Pages 43L, p49C

Josephine Coatsworth
Pages 39L, 39R, 49TR, 50L, 52, 53, 55L, 57R, 58L, 64R, 71R, 72, 81C, 83L, 88C, 90R.

Stan Farwig
Pages 5, 40R, 47L, 56L, 61L, 64L, 65L, 69R, 70L, 73TR, 74L, 75L, 79L, 84C, 84R, 90L, 93B.

Derek Fell
Pages 15, 41L, 42L, 49L, 50R, 54, 58R, 62L, 77L, 77R, 78L, 79R, 81R, 82L, 83C, 86L, 88L, 91L, 91C, 91R.

Grant Heilman Photography
Page 6.

Saxon Holt
Pages 35, 45L, 59R, 66.

Sandra F. Ladendorf
Pages 18, 88R.

Michael Landis
Pages 14, 27, 48L, 80.

Richard W. Lighty, Director
Pages 46L, 51R, 86BR.

Lee Lockwood
Pages 11, 20B.

Michael McKinley
Pages 34, 44L, 45R, 48C, 68R, 73L, 73BR.

James K. McNair
Pages 38, 51L, 70R.

Malek Photographs Ltd.
Front Cover, Title Page, Pages 4, 12, 16, 17, 24, Back Cover.

Brian Matthew
Pages 42R, 69L.

Fred Meier
Page 7.

Jack Napton
Page 89L.

Ortho Library
Page 13, 25, 71L, 71C, 92L.

Park Seed Co.
Page 21.

Pam Peirce
Pages 20T, 22T, 23, 29, 37R, 43R, 55R, 56R, 57TL, 57B, 60R, 65R, 67, 68L, 85L, 85R, 86TR, 93T.

Picnic Productions
Page 22B.

Roger Raische
Pages 62R, 89R.

Wayne Roderick
Pages 41R, 75L, 81L, 84L, 87R.

Susan Roth
Page 76.

Michael D. Smith
Page 36.

Stark Studios
Page 83R.

Thompson and Morgan
Pages 41C, 92R.

Tom Tracy
Page 37L.

M. van Waveren and Sons, Mount Airy, NC and International Bloembollencentrum, Holland.
Pages 40L, 47R, 59L, 60L, 61R, 63, 74TR, 74BR, 87L.

Michael Willets
Page 44R.

Flower arrangement on page 23 by Bloomers San Francisco, California

Special Thanks

B & D Lilies
Port Townsend, Oregon

Mitchell Beauchamp

Conservatory of Flowers, Golden Gate Park
San Francisco, California

Tom Courtright
Orchard Nursery and Florist
Lafayette, California

Denise Dirickson
Pier 39, San Francisco, California.

Paul Doty
Berkeley Horticultural Nursery
Berkeley, California

David Goldberg

Iris Goldman and Doug Brentlinger

James J. Lang

Harold and Susan Muller

Potrero Gardens Nursery
San Francisco, California

John J. Sabuco
Good Earth Company
Flossmoor, Illinois

Anthony Skittone
San Francisco, California

David J.A. Smith
White Flower Farm
Litchfield, Connecticut

Strybing Arboretum
San Francisco, California

Pat Taylor

Western Hills Nursery
Occidental, California

Jim Wilson

All About Bulbs

A trick for making eye-catching displays: Select two bulbs with the same flower color. These are Triumph tulip 'Dreaming Maid' and hyacinth 'Amsterdam'.

Bulbs: Concentrated Beauty

A bulb contains a complete flower, along with all the food it needs to bloom. Just add water . . .

The snow is only beginning to melt when winter-weary gardeners are heartened by the earliest crocuses and winter aconites. Soon other bulbs fill garden areas with bursts of floral sunshine in a celebration of spring. Many weeks later, when bearded irises are waning and summer languor is settling on the garden, pots and hanging baskets of tuberous begonias cool the patio with their sherbet tints, and spires of lilies preside over lightly shaded borders.

Still later when weeks of heat sear the garden and diminish its variety and color, the belladonna lily springs out of bare earth into full bloom, renewing fragrance and brilliance in the garden. Colchicums and autumn crocuses prefigure nippy nights and waning days, but just when the first heavy storms of winter bury the last cyclamens and force even the hardiest gardener indoors, a burst of hyacinths makes a perfumed island of springtime on a windowsill.

Bulb plants embody the loveliest qualities of all the seasons—not just the brightness of spring, for which they are famous. Their clear colors warm our hearts with their glow. At close range, the petals of most bulb flowers are, like orchid petals, aggregates of tiny glistening jewels. Some bulb flowers are satiny, others waxy, others crepelike or mat. Some are flashy showstoppers; others modestly wait for their subtle charms to be discovered.

Something For Everybody

All About Bulbs is written for everyone who appreciates the unique beauty of bulbs, from the accomplished gardener to the person whose gardening experience consists solely of bringing a gift pot of crocuses into flower. Included here for the novice gardener are the most basic planting and care instructions for growing popular and best-loved bulbs.

Experienced bulb gardeners will find some advanced techniques that allow them to grow bulbs that they thought wouldn't grow in their area and to enjoy bulbs outside the normal blooming season. They will also find scores of unusual bulbs, including exotic beauties seldom discussed in gardening literature. Some of these rare bulbs are difficult to locate, so the addresses of bulb specialists are provided (see page 26).

A close inspection of *Babiana ambigua* reveals a scattering of jewellike sparkles on the petals.

Trout lilies (*Erythronium americanum*) are native to the forests of eastern North America. As you might expect, they do best with shade, an acid soil, and cold winters. If you have a wooded garden in a wet-summer, cold-winter area, trout lilies will naturalize and can be grown with a minimum of care.

On the whole, bulbs are the most remarkably adaptable and undemanding of flowers, as long as a few basic guidelines, which are included here, are followed.

This chapter examines all types of bulbs, including true bulbs, corms, tubers, tuberous roots, and rhizomes. It also explores major bulb regions around the world and the environmental factors that have encouraged plants to evolve into bulbs. One of the guidelines to growing any plant successfully is knowing what that plant "expects," that is, the conditions to which it has adapted. To a large extent the temperature and rainfall patterns and the soil and sunlight conditions of a bulb's native habitat determine its cultural needs.

The second chapter is full of ideas for using bulbs. It explains how to lay out borders, beds, and formal plantings. You'll also find design ideas for garden meadows, woodlands, and gardens. Those special spots beneath sheltering eaves or in chinks in rock walls and stone paving are perfect for certain bulbs.

Bulbs are well-suited for containers, raised beds, and trough gardens. For the enthusiastic bulb gardener, there are ideas for extending the range of bulbs that can be grown by using special structures—from a simple bulb frame to a more elaborate alpine- or greenhouse.

You'll also find tips for using bulbs indoors—as year-round houseplants, as potted plants that are brought indoors only when they are in bloom, and as cut flowers. Complete instructions are included for forcing bulbs, that is, getting them to bloom in the winter.

The third chapter tells how to buy, plant, and care for bulbs—practical information that enables you to bring your bulbs into bloom not just the first season but repeatedly, maintaining their health and vigor and increasing their numbers.

The "Directory of Bulbs" is an encyclopedia of both popular bulbs and those that deserve to be popular but aren't yet. It tells you where each bulb comes from, where it will grow, what conditions it needs to thrive, and specific tips for growing and using each bulb.

Native Habitats Of Bulbs

Most of the plants in this book share a solution to an environmental problem. They use a relatively brief period of good weather to store energy (in the form of starch) in an underground "bank," then become dormant during a relatively long period of adverse weather. When the adverse period is past, they invest the energy in rapid growth and flowering. Although bulbs have originated in several different climates, the majority of them have come from areas with Mediterranean climates.

Mediterranean Climates. In the Mediterranean region and a few other regions of winter rain and summer drought, bulbs store nourishment to sustain the plants during the dry months and to launch a season of flowering. In some locales, such as the high meadows of the Caucasus, the interval between snowmelt and searing heat is brief. In such locations, underground storage organs provide readily available food, which enables the plants to flower as quickly as possible and produce leaves to gather energy for the next bloom season. A crocus or daffodil native to such an environment sprouts flowers, produces foliage, withers, and lapses into dormancy all within a few weeks. Brought into cultivation, the plant retains its need for fall rains, winter chilling, spring dampness, and summer drought conditions that, as you will learn in the next chapter, are relatively easy to provide, even in areas with heavy summer rainfall.

Other regions with Mediterranean climates provide a longer season of flowers and leaves, but even in those regions, bulbs, corms, rhizomes, or tubers are a means of surviving climatic extremes, particularly a long season of drought and heat. Most of these bulbs have coverings that help prevent drying. Many bulbs that have evolved under such conditions require a cool, rainy season in which to grow, followed by a hot, dry season in which to rest. In the garden, summer rainfall or watering encourages bulb-rotting diseases. Fortunately, however, most of the cultivated bulbs that originated in Mediterranean climate areas tolerate summer rainfall if they are planted in soil that drains well. You will notice in the "Directory of Bulbs" that the most common cultural need of bulbs is well-drained soil.

The rainy winter, dry summer weather pattern of the Mediterranean area extends from southern Europe to Asia Minor and the interior of Asia. Most species of narcissus, tulip, crocus, hyacinth, and grape hyacinth, as well as many other spring-blooming bulbs, have their origins in this large area. Other areas of the world with Mediterranean climates are parts of South Africa (home of more bulb species than any other area of the world), California, western and southern Australia, and Chile.

Wet-Summer, Dry-Winter Climates. South Africa offers a perfect example of the need to know something about the original habitat of plants. The southwestern part of the country, home of the greatest concentration of bulbs in the world, has the typical Mediterranean climate described above, but the remainder has cool, bright, dry winters and wet summers. Bulbs from either area usually require an approximation of the same conditions when they are grown elsewhere. For example, one group of gladiolus species is from the Mediterranean climate of South Africa and demands one cultural regimen if left in the garden year around; another group is from South African areas of dry winters and wet summers and calls for another regimen. Because so many bulbs are native to South Africa, its climate patterns are especially significant to bulb growers.

This climate pattern is also found in parts of tropical Africa and South America.

Tropical Climates With Year-Round Rain. Over much of the tropics (including some high-elevation areas that never get very hot), rain falls in every season, though often with enough seasonal variation that bulbs native to those areas have periods of active growth and periods of relative dormancy. Typically—but by no means always—they are evergreen or semideciduous, and in cultivation must never be allowed to dry out completely. Most of them grow in well-drained soils that, like woodland soils of the temperate zones, contain a high percentage of decayed organic matter. Many of the bulbs that are commonly grown as houseplants, such as clivia, eucharis, and worsleya, are from these tropical regions that have rainfall in every season.

Cold-Winter, Wet-Summer Climates. Except for parts of the West and Southeast, the United States generally has a pattern of cold winters—during which nearly all precipitation is snow—and warm, rainy summers. Many of the lilies come from this area and from similar climate areas of Asia. Arisaemas, erythroniums, trilliums, and bluebells come from similar environments in North America, Asia, or Europe. These bulbs are woodland plants requiring summer moisture, deep acid soil full of decayed organic matter, and good drainage. Some blossom and leaf out in the gentle spring sun, ahead of the deciduous trees that overshadow them, then luxuriate in the cool, moist, but never wet, soil beneath the woodland canopy through the heat of summer. In the garden their winter dormancy allows digging and storage throughout the cold winter months where necessary. Often winter mulching suffices to protect them from freezing and from the damaging effects of alternately freezing and then thawing.

Hippeastrum puniceum, an ancestor of our modern amaryllis *(Hippeastrum),* growing in a Peruvian jungle. Bulbs from tropical areas prefer a peaty soil that drains quickly and is never allowed to dry out. Many, but not this one, are evergreen.

What Is a Bulb?

For simplicity, we apply the word *bulb* to all plants that store energy for their seasonal cycle in an underground storage organ. Actually, only some of these plants are true bulbs, but the underground storage organs of all of them serve the same general functions.

All bulbous plants store food to carry them through a dormant period. Dormancy is one of nature's many solutions to getting through a time of difficult weather conditions. In nature, dormancy is brought on naturally by winter's cold or summer's drought. In some climates, however, it is necessary for the gardener to enforce dormancy by withholding water or by digging up and storing the bulb.

True Bulbs. Of the plants described in this book, only about half are true bulbs. A true bulb is a package of fleshy scales containing a small basal plate and a shoot. If you slice vertically through a tulip bulb at planting time, you can see a complete miniature plant with tiny flowers, stem, leaves, and roots.

The scales surrounding the embryo are modified leaves that contain all the necessary food to sustain the bulb during dormancy and early growth. The scales may be loose and open, like those of a lily, or tight and compact, like those of a hyacinth. If a tight bulb is cut in half crosswise, the scales are visible as rings.

Around the scales, many bulbs have a paper-thin covering known as the *tunic*. At the bottom of the bulb is a modified stem, or *basal plate*, from which the roots emerge. The basal plate also holds the scales together. During the growing season, new bulbs (called *bulblets* or *offsets*) are formed from lateral buds on the basal plates. Lilies can also form stem bulblets. With some bulbs, such as tulips, the old bulb dies, leaving the new ones. With other bulbs, such as narcissus, the parent continues to grow and bulblets can be separated from it to create new plants. A few bulbs, such as some species of lilies, form new *bulbils* in the leaf axils; these bulbils can be used for propagation.

True Bulbs.
True Bulbs are composed of modified leaves. The individual leaves are seen as scales, as in lilies, or rings, as in daffodils and tulips.

Bulbils on a lily stem.

From left to right: daffodil (this one is a *double-nosed* bulb), lily, tulip.

Parts of a tulip bulb.

Tunic

Scales

Bud

Bulblet

Basal plate

Corms. A corm is actually a stem that is modified into a mass of storage tissue. If a corm is cut in half crosswise, no rings are visible. The top of the corm has one or more growing points, or eyes, which are usually visible on close examination. Corms are covered by dry leaf bases much like the tunics that cover many true bulbs, but there are no enlarged scales. Roots grow from a basal plate on the underside of the corm. As the plant grows, the corm shrivels away. New corms form on top of or beside the old one. In addition, some corms, such as gladiolus, form *cormels*, or tiny corms.

The large corms will produce flowers the following year, but it takes two to three years for cormels to produce blossoms.

Tubers. The tuber is a solid underground mass of stem similar to the corm, but it lacks both a basal plate and the tuniclike covering of the corm. Roots and shoots grow from growth buds, or eyes, scattered over the surface. As the plants grow, some tubers, such as those of caladiums, diminish in size and new tubers, such as those of ranunculuses, form others, increase in size as they store nutrients, and develop new growth buds for the following year.

How Bulbs Multiply

Offsets, also called **splits** or **spoons,** develop within the mother bulb, then break away to form new plants.

Bulblets are offsets that develop just above or below the mother bulb.

Bulbils are tiny bulbs that form along the stem, above ground. Several lilies, including tiger lilies, produce bulbils.

Cormels are offsets that are produced around the edge of a corm during the growing season. Some gladiolus can produce up to 50 cormels.

Pips are underground rootstalks, or shoots, produced by rhizomes. Lily-of-the-valley is usually propagated in this way.

Corms.
Corms are composed of modified stem tissue. They have no rings or scales.

Tubers.
Like corms, tubers are developed from stem tissue.

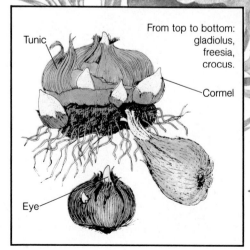

Tunic

From top to bottom: gladiolus, freesia, crocus.

Cormel

Eye

From top to bottom: potato, gloriosa lily, ranunculus, anemone.

Eyes

Rhizomes. Sometimes known as *rootstock*, rhizomes are actually thickened, branching storage stems. They grow laterally just along or slightly below the surface of the soil. However, some plants—such as trilliums—have rhizomes several inches deep.

Roots develop on the lower surface, and buds along the top of the rhizome produce the new plants during the growing season. Rhizomes may be propagated by cutting the parent plant into sections. But, each segment must contain a bud.

Although the various bulbous plants have their distinct differences, the common factor is their ability to store food to carry them over a period of adverse weather conditions until their above-ground growth begins again. This "dormancy" may be brought on naturally by winter or drought in moderate-temperature climates. However, it may be neces-sary to enforce dormancy by withholding moisture or removing the bulbs from the ground.

Tuberous Roots. These nutrient storage units look like tubers but are really swollen roots. During growth, they produce fibrous roots to take in moisture and nutrients. New growth buds appear on the base of the old stem, where it joins the tuberous root. Roots can be divided by cutting off a section with an eye-bearing portion from where the old stem was attached.

Tuberous Roots.
These look like tubers, but are developed from root tissue.

Rhizomes.
These are horizontal stems or runners.

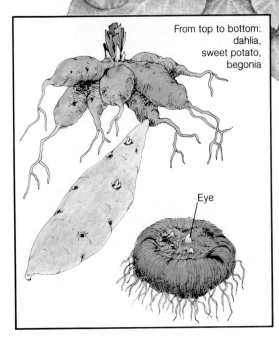

From top to bottom: dahlia, sweet potato, begonia

Eye

Left: Iris
Right: Convallaria

Eye

Pip

New Developments With Bulbs

Much that has been said thus far in this chapter concerns the origins of bulbs—the native habitats of wild species. Yet most of the bulbs grown by home gardeners are hybrids of these lovely wildings. Hybridizers have in many instances gilded a modest species by magnifying its size, multiplying its colors, and extending its forms. They have also created widely adaptable, easy-to-grow garden flowers from sometimes exacting or difficult wild forms. The most successful of these hybrids are marketed all over the world. The Netherlands leads the way in modern bulb production, followed by England, the United States, and Japan.

A brief look at the Dutch bulb industry reveals an intensity of hybridization and scientific research that is causing tremendous changes in our home gardens. Countless new varieties have been produced by a few Dutch families, companies, and scientists who have spent generations cross-pollinating flowers and nursing their progeny. This time-consuming process involves removing pollen-producing stamens from one variety and brushing them against the pollen-receptive stigma of another variety. Out of thousands of crosses, one new variety may be accepted as superior to existing varieties.

Once a new hybrid has been selected, it may take as long as fifteen years to produce enough bulbs from the original parent to present the new variety to the Dutch Bulb Jury. This body, which meets each Monday at the Bloembollencentrum (Flower-Bulb Center) in Hillegom, has the task of deciding which new varieties are worthy of being introduced into commerce. The jury's stamp of approval means that the producer can proceed to develop enough bulbs to offer in the marketplace in a few years. The complexity of creating new bulb varieties explains why high prices are charged for new hybrids. As more bulbs become available, the prices begin to fall.

In the Netherlands a number of bulb producers are currently exploring revolutionary methods of hybridizing. The Institute for Horticultural Plant Breeding is experimenting with exposing bulbs to virus-carrying aphids, nitrous oxide, and X-rays to create mutations under highly controlled conditions. These new methods have produced flowers of sometimes remarkably transformed appearance at a far faster rate than the traditional methods. In spite of these experiments, most Dutch bulb producers still rely on old-fashioned luck and keen observation to develop beautiful new hybrids.

Hybridization of bulbs is by no means limited to the Netherlands. For example, the world center of lily hybridization is Oregon, where, in just a few years, Jan de Graaff and other hybridizers have vastly increased the number of lily varieties and created new looks in lilies. Many of the hybrids adapt more easily than their ancestors to a wide range of growing conditions. In addition to commercial hybridizers, members of bulb societies create scores of hybrids annually. The result of all bulb hybridization is not just a wider range of beautiful flowers but also easier and more adaptable bulbs for every home gardener.

Bulb fields near Lisse, in the Netherlands. Because of the near-perfect climate and rich soil, raising flower bulbs has become a major industry in the Netherlands, where high-tech horticultural techniques are often combined with age-old methods.

The strongest
design statement is
made by a large
planting of a single
variety, as in this
border of 'Golden
Wedding' tulips.

In the Garden
And in the House

These adaptable flowers can be used in landscapes, lath houses, and containers. They can be brought indoors as forced winter blooms, houseplants, or cut flowers.

Bulbs adapt to a myriad of settings. Imagine drifts of daffodils and snowdrops meandering through a small garden meadow of grass and annual wildflowers, or lush clumps of trilliums nestling beneath deciduous trees among random patches of forget-me-nots and woodland ferns. Imagine cheery pink-flowered tufts of rhodohypoxis bursting from cracks between flagstones in a garden walkway, or symmetrical patterns of yellow tulips of precisely the same height, underplanted with blue violas and surrounded by a low hedge of dwarf box. Imagine a diminutive clump of tecophilaea with its indigo-blue flowers sparkling in a rock-garden niche, entryway planters displaying clusters of red-orange clivia blossoms among dark green leaves, or large and small dahlias running riot among the bright perennials of a summer border.

This chapter will help you discover dozens of new ways to use bulbs in your garden and in your home. But it aims even higher—to help you broaden the scope of your bulb plantings by augmenting your garden's natural growing conditions. This can be useful in any climate area, but is especially useful where the climate or soil is inhospitable to many bulbs. Although not every bulb grows well in every garden, your garden may offer far more possibilities than you think.

Formal Plantings

Only a few bulbs lend themselves to formal plantings, but these can create some striking effects. The classic bulbs for formal plantings are tulips, usually planted in large numbers of the same variety. They are particularly effective when underplanted with other flowers in contrasting or complementary colors. Violas, grape hyacinths, alyssums, wallflowers, forget-me-nots, candytufts, and primulas are all used for underplanting.

Formal plantings are costly and difficult, but stunning. The effect comes partially from the uniformity and precision of the planting. To achieve this precision, new bulbs of a uniform size must be bought each year. The bed must be excavated and leveled, the bulbs set precisely in place and covered, and then the companion flowers planted.

Massed to accentuate the erectness, density, and uniformity of their spikes, garden hyacinths are particularly effective in formal beds. Daffodils, Dutch irises, or bearded irises can also be used for formal spring displays; and lilies, dwarf cannas, or the larger alliums are good for summer displays.

A formal effect can also be achieved with identical containers of bulbs arranged symmetrically—for example, matching urns of tulips flanking steps or a walkway. But in most gardens, bulbs are easier to use and more appropriate in an informal setting.

A densely planted tray of daffodils makes a portable accent that can be used anyplace in the garden. These are 'Joseph MacLeon'.

Drifts of naturalized daffodils bloom in a meadow garden. After the foliage has yellowed, the meadow will be mowed and become a lawn.

Garden Meadows

A garden meadow is a lawn left unmowed until midsummer when patches of spring crocuses, calochortuses, reticulata irises, snowdrops, anemones, daffodils, brodiaeas, or other spring bulbs can bloom and then ripen their foliage. Bulbs that are adapted to the region will naturalize; plantings are more or less permanent, and bulbs multiply over the years, expanding in natural drifts.

A permanent meadow (one that doesn't become a lawn for the summer) can include wildflowers and wild grasses that keep the area colorful for a long time and hide the withering bulb foliage. This type of meadow is mowed once a year—usually in midsummer— and takes little further care. If the plants are adapted to your region, they don't need summer water, and fertilizing isn't necessary once the meadow is established. Colchicums and autumn crocuses can renew the flowering-meadow effect after vegetation has been mowed in midsummer.

A sloping or uneven area with good drainage is most suitable.

The bulbs look best planted in clumps and loose drifts. One way of planting is to throw out a handful of bulbs, then plant each where it falls. For a small-scale, easy-maintenance meadow of small bulbs, consider using, instead of grass, a ground cover such as chamomile or yarrow, which looks at home in a meadow, requires little or no summer watering, and remains—or can be mowed—short.

Woodland Gardens

Another "wild" garden is the woodland garden, where a wide range of bulbs look at home and can naturalize. Deciduous trees, before they leaf out, allow the bulbs plenty of sun for blooming and ripening of foliage. The soil tends to be acid in most woodlands. Soil that is too acid can be "sweetened" with limestone, as explained on page 28. Many of the species described in the "Directory of Bulbs" are woodland natives adapted to growing under trees. In fact, because the tree canopy deflects summer rain and tree roots help keep the soil dry, woodland gardens suit most spring-blooming bulbs, and a number of summer- and fall-blooming ones as well.

Some of the spring-blooming bulbs that thrive in woodland gardens are trilliums, bluebells, arisaemas, chionodoxas, eranthises, galanthuses, lilies-of-the-valley, some tulip species, crested irises, daffodils, erythroniums, some fritillarias, and most grape hyacinths. Summer-blooming bulbs for woodland gardens include some lilies, some alliums, and the spectacular cardiocrinum. All should be positioned carefully according to the amount of light they need because few thrive in deep shade, and some demand lots of sun. Autumn-flowering bulbs for woodlands include some of the cyclamen species, colchicums, autumn-flowering crocuses, and zephyranthes.

In order to create a woodland garden, you don't need acres of woodland, or even a large grove. As few as two or three deciduous trees can help provide the shade and refreshing atmosphere of a woodland.

Borders

When we think of bulbs in the home garden we usually think of borders. The English, those masters of garden borders, distinguish between borders and beds. Borders are at edges of gardens, against walls or hedges, and beds are elsewhere. Beds are often thought of as containing organized plantings of bedding plants, and borders are mixed or less formal. In this book *borders* refers to both beds and borders, except where a distinction is important. In most respects, beds and borders are identical. Borders can be herbaceous (all flowers) or mixed (containing both flowers and shrubs). Bulbs have an important place in both.

In mixed borders, where a backbone of shrubs is complemented by a seasonal succession of perennial flowers, there is little digging. This means that bulbs can be planted and, with luck, escape the depredations of the shovel. In herbaceous borders, particularly those containing annuals, there is inevitably more cultivating and digging, so it's necessary to mark the locations of dormant bulbs.

Bulbs in herbaceous and mixed borders must usually be able to grow in rich soil, perhaps with fertilizing and summer watering. Many of the modern hybrids—lilies, bearded irises, tulips, narcissus, and dahlias, for example—have been bred to flourish under a wide range of garden conditions. Many natural species accept richness and summer moisture, too—such as crown fritillarias and the ornithogalums. Other species can be used in spots where there is little or no feeding and scant summer watering—for example, corydalis among perennials and species cyclamen among shrubs.

Successful border gardening is largely a matter—and a challenging one—of planting so that pleasing combinations of flowers bloom simultaneously and are succeeded by others. Using bulbs in the border makes this easier.

Rock Gardens

Rock gardens are not merely a beautiful setting for many bulbs, but, among ever-increasing numbers of gardeners, a way of life. The American Rock Garden Society is only one of the gardening groups devoted to the art of rock gardening. As a wider range of plants becomes better known to home gardeners, rock gardens will undoubtedly become more common in the United States.

What is a rock garden? In short, it is a sloping garden with rocks and gritty soil. To some extent it replicates the natural environment of alpine plants—plants from mountainous or rocky terrains. Many have brief but spectacular periods of spring bloom and then become dormant during the hot, dry summer.

As discussed in the previous chapter, climates with a brief growing season followed by a long period of adverse weather foster the evolution of bulbs. Many bulbs thrive in alpine conditions. These can be planted in rock gardens as specimens or, more often, in clumps or drifts. Most rock gardens are situated for maximum sun exposure, although they usually provide some sheltered sites (behind rocks, in crevices, or on north-facing slopes, for example) for plants that require shade. Alpine plants have evolved in environments where compact growth is a survival advantage, and many are small. Some plants, including many bulbs that look and grow best in rock gardens, aren't alpine in their origins but still thrive in rock gardens because of the quick drainage.

Rock garden soils usually contain generous proportions of sand, grit, and even gravel, together with organic material such as peat moss. In a rock garden, a gravel or grit mulch looks natural, discourages weeds, and keeps crowns and lower leaves of moisture-sensitive alpine plants from rotting. It also keeps blossoms from being splashed with mud.

Rock gardens are usually raised above the natural grade. The elevation of a rock garden not only helps drainage, but also displays the compact plants closer to eye level than flat beds do. For instance, *Crocus speciosus* viewed close-up reveals exquisite patterns of purple feathering.

Garden spots that aren't strictly parts of a rock garden can meet the needs of rock garden plants and display them to great advantage. For example, crocus, grape hyacinth, oxalis, and scilla—nearly any diminutive spring-flowering bulb—are charming growing in cracks around the flagstones. Pockets of gritty soil between the stones give them the footing they need, and they will like the heat retained by the flagstones. Alpine bulbs also thrive at the sunny base of a rock wall or even in the chinks between the rocks of a dry-laid (unmortared) wall.

All of the miniature, hardy spring- and summer-flowering bulbs, including the small alliums, Greek anemones, most tulip species, and the miniature early bulbs recommended above for meadow and woodland gardens are appropriate for rock gardens and other spots that afford them rock-garden conditions. In the Mediterranean-climate areas of California,

Although the effect here is of a mixed border, the tulips are planted in their own bed in front of the shrubs. When their season is finished, they can be easily overplanted with annuals. The tulip is 'Beauty of Apeldoorn'.

Raised beds are easier to care for, and they bring the flowers up to eye (and nose) level for better visibility and appreciation. The tulip in front is 'Lustige Witwe'.

rock gardens make cultivation of scores of winter-growing, summer-dry bulbs easy, because drainage is fast, and mild winters and dry summers allow them to stay in the ground the year around. These bulbs include ixias, freesias, geissorhizas, romuleas, calochortuses, brodiaeas, babianas, winter-growing gladiolus, many moraeas, and *Bulbinella floribunda*.

Raised Beds and Miniature Gardens

Raised beds share two advantages with rock gardens. Because they are raised above the level of surrounding ground, they offer rapid drainage even where the native soil drains poorly. And, like a well-designed rock garden, raised beds bring plants closer to eye and hand level for greater enjoyment and easier tending.

The miniature garden is a raised bed on a small scale. It is usually naturalistic and can make a complete landscape in even the tiniest courtyard. Miniature gardens first became popular as trough gardens, made in an old stone sink or trough. These are now nearly impossible to find—and expensive if you succeed—but a concrete or enamel sink with adequate drainage will function as well, even if it doesn't look as good. Assure quick drainage by heaping large potsherds over the drainage holes, then making a layer of rocks or smaller potsherds, a layer of coarse sphagnum moss, and a top layer of light soil. Along with other suitable plants—saxifraga and dwarf wallflower, for example—you might plant bulbs such as reticulata iris, species cyclamen, crocus, rhodohypoxis, the smaller chionodoxa, grape hyacinth, and the smallest species of allium and daffodil. If you have no space even for a miniature garden, consider adapting the idea to a window box, using small bulbs for a garden to be enjoyed at close

range or larger, bolder bulbs to be enjoyed also by passersby.

Containers

Flowerpots or bulb pans (broad, shallow pots), small wooden boxes or large tubs, and other simple or decorative containers offer distinct advantages for growing bulbs outdoors. (Containers are also indispensable for growing bulbs indoors and within various enclosures, subjects explored later in this chapter and in the next.)

Even in climate areas where a wide range of bulbs can be grown the year around in borders and rock gardens, many of the most sophisticated gardeners prefer containers for their prize specimens. Many bulbs accept crowding, and some grow and bloom better for being crowded in a container—for example, agapanthus and clivia. With suitable soil and adequate drainage holes, a container drains quickly. Bulbs in containers are safe from gophers, moles, and other rodents. The portability of containers allows you to move them into view when the bulbs are flowering, to a hot spot for baking during the dormancy period, or into shelter over a cold winter.

Shelters for Bulbs

Perhaps the summer sun in your area is too intense for some of the bulbs that you want to grow, or the winters are too cold for tender bulbs. Perhaps summer rains prevent you from growing summer-dormant bulbs that need dryness, or winter rains interfere with growing bulbs that need dry winters. You can overcome these problems by providing shelters. Even a simple shelter can expand the range of bulbs you can raise. Some bulbs won't need to remain in the shelters the year around, but just during the seasons when they need protection.

Lath Houses. Wherever the summer sun is too hot for bulbs, the simple, old-fashioned lath house is the perfect answer. Even in mild coastal climates, tuberous begonias look better if they're grown under lath. So do other bulbs whose natural habitats are shady.

A lath house is an enclosure roofed with lath. The laths are usually spaced about their own width, so the bands of sun and shade are the same width. They are set closer where the sun is particularly hot, and farther apart in milder climates. Laths should run north and south, so that bands of sun don't linger too long in one spot.

Alpine Houses and Bulb Frames. An alpine house is an unheated greenhouse used to grow bulbs and alpine plants. A bulb frame is a high cold frame dedicated to bulbs. A typical alpine house accommodates lots of bulbs, including tall-growing ones such as dierama and large-scale gladiolus; a typical bulb frame accommodates fewer and smaller bulbs (which most bulbs are). A bulb frame usually represents a more modest expense and effort than an alpine house. Otherwise, these two shelters are functionally identical, or nearly so.

Containers of bulbs can be moved around a garden much as furniture can be moved around a room. Use containers for special effects, to create an ever-changing focus in a display area, or to add spots of color during drab seasons.

This British alpine house is an unheated greenhouse with a row of ventilating windows at bench level. Alpine houses make it possible to grow Mediterranean-climate bulbs in wet-summer areas.

A bulb frame is essentially a raised bed of bulbs with a glass cover; the bulbs may grow in containers rather than the ground. Glass panels adjust for ventilation, and lift off easily.

An alpine house is similar. It may be thought of as a walk-in bulb frame or an unheated greenhouse with particularly good ventilation. Like a frame it may contain bulbs in pots or in raised beds. Or, it may be meticulously landscaped—a display rock garden under glass.

Either kind of shelter makes growing Mediterranean-climate bulbs possible in regions with rainy summers. It also allows northern gardeners to raise such winter-growing bulbs as freesias, ixias, romuleas, geissorhizas, calochortuses, hesperanthas, brodiaeas, many of the moraeas, and *Bulbinella floribunda*. An unheated shelter is also a safe place to cultivate spring- or summer-growing bulbs that are not hardy in the open garden. In some regions where semihardy bulbs survive winter in the open garden but aren't robust, they perform beautifully in an unheated shelter. Even some of the hardiest bulbs are susceptible to damage from late frosts and thus benefit from the protection of an alpine house or a bulb frame. Bulbs

being forced (see page 19), as well as seedlings and newly planted offsets (see page 30), do better in a shelter.

Perhaps setting up even a bulb frame is a larger project than you want to take on. If you need a separate shelter for a small group of bulbs, perhaps to bake them during their dormancy, try *cloches* (literally "bells"): miniature lift-off tents. You can improvise them, using fiberglass or plastic sheeting over a wood or wire framework. Leave holes near the top to ventilate them when the sun is out.

Greenhouses. Heated greenhouses greatly expand the gardener's scope. They protect their contents from the natural elements and provide whatever heat and humidity the plants need. Greenhouses are useful for growing bulbs in most climates, and indispensable for growing many kinds of bulbs in cold-winter regions.

A cool greenhouse, whose thermostat is set at just above freezing, is the perfect environment for bulbs that do their growing during a cool, rainy winter and early spring. Some examples are given above, in the discussion of alpine houses and bulb frames. But a cool, well-

ventilated greenhouse can do everything an alpine house or a bulb frame can, and it can do it in the coldest regions.

A warm greenhouse is the ideal environment for tender and semihardy bulbs, including many of the bulbs commonly grown as houseplants. Some of the bulbs that thrive in a warm greenhouse (though not all require identical conditions) are clivia, achimenes, gloxinia, tigridia, eucomis, Scarborough lily, crinum, sprekelia, eucharis, gloriosa, and worsleya. Greenhouses are also useful for forcing bulbs, a process described in the next chapter.

Bulbs Indoors

Bulbs are among the easiest flowers to grow indoors. Their colors, forms, and scents bring concentrated outdoor beauty into the house—especially welcome in winter when the garden is at its nadir. Some tropical and subtropical bulbs can be grown as houseplants and kept indoors all or much of the year. Others can be grown outdoors in containers and brought inside when they bloom. And some hardy bulbs can be forced to bloom before their normal season in the garden and kept indoors while they are in bloom. In addition, bulbs provide some of the choicest cut flowers for the house throughout the year.

Bulbs That Can Be Grown Indoors All Year

Achimenes	Hippeastrum
Agapanthus	Hymenocallis
Begonia	Milla
Caladium	Ornithogalum
Canna	Oxalis
Chlidanthus	Pancratium
Clivia	Polianthes
Crinum	Sinningia
Cyclamen persicum	Smithiantha
	Sprekelia
Cyrtanthus	Tulbaghia
Eucharis	Veltheimia
Eucomis	Worsleya
Freesia	Zantedeschia
Gloriosa	

Bulbs as Houseplants. Many tropical and semitropical bulbs make splendid houseplants. Most thrive in the same temperatures that people find comfortable. Some are deciduous; others are evergreen or semievergreen. Those listed on the previous page are excellent houseplants. In addition to the plants in this list, it's fun to experiment with growing bulbs such as Greek anemone and zephyranthes. Try to approximate the conditions under which they thrive in gardens. Move their pots from cooler to warmer parts of the house when seasonal temperature changes are called for, and increase or decrease watering and decrease or stop feeding bulbs that have dormant periods.

At each watering, add enough water so that some drains into the saucer. This flushes salts from the soil so they don't accumulate to a damaging level. After the pot is through draining, empty the saucer. Wait until the soil is just barely moist—not wet and not dry—before watering again. When a bulb is actively growing, it needs regular watering. When it's dormant, it only needs occasional dampening.

The soil should drain within minutes after watering. If it doesn't, the soil is too compact, and the bulb should be repotted. Most commercial potting mixes are good for growing bulbs. As a precaution against excess salts in the mix, water the plant several times as soon as you repot it. If you prefer to make your own mix, use 1 part coarse sand, 1 part peat moss, and 1 part sawdust or ground bark. Add 1 tablespoon of ground limestone and 1 tablespoon of superphosphate per quart of mix.

Like other houseplants, bulbs thrive on frequent, light feedings. A good method is to feed at every watering, with one fourth the recommended amount of fertilizer.

Stop feeding completely during dormancy periods. Let the soil become almost dry, then add just

enough water to moisten it (an exception to the rule that you should always add enough water so that some drains into the saucer).

Bulbs like a higher humidity than is normal in most homes. Place bulbs away from heaters and air ducts and raise the humidity around them with a humidifier, either the type that is built into the furnace or a portable type that can be placed near the plants. You can raise the humidity a little by grouping bulbs together and placing them in trays of pebbles with water in the bottom. Don't let the pots touch the water.

Most bulb houseplants are native to tropical forests. They grow best in bright but not direct sunlight. If you want to place them in a sunny window, screen it with a gauze curtain. All bulbs need more light to bloom than to produce healthy leaves. For more flowers, give them as much light as they can tolerate without bleaching the leaves yellow.

Pots of Bulbs From the Garden. Whenever they bloom in the garden, container-grown bulbs can be brought indoors. All garden bulbs are suitable for this purpose. Any bulb that flourishes in a container outdoors can come

A pot of blooming bulbs, such as these 'King Alfred' daffodils, can be used in much the same way as a flower arrangement—to grace special occasions or brighten a family lunch.

indoors, at least for a while, during its blooming. Hide clay pots with a cachepot or basket.

Care of these visitors is essentially the same as that of bulbs grown as houseplants. But because these bulbs have been shifted abruptly from outdoors, they are especially sensitive to inhospitable indoor conditions. If they are to remain longer than a few days, situate them in bright light. However, the blossoms will last longer if they don't receive full sun. Most bulbs can be left indoors until the blooms are past their peak. If they are outdoor bulbs that flower for a long period, though, don't keep them indoors for more than two or three weeks. If they remain indoors too long, especially with inadequate light, they will have trouble readjusting to garden conditions.

Forcing Bulbs Indoors

Stimulating a plant to bloom out of season is called *forcing*. Forced bulbs can provide winter color in your home from Christmas until spring. Most gardeners force bulbs for displaying in pots, but you can also force blooms close together in flats if you want to grow flowers for cutting.

The bulbs most commonly forced are daffodils, tulips, hyacinths, and crocuses. Others that can easily be forced include galanthuses, Dutch and reticulata irises, grape hyacinths, ornithogalums, eranthises, brodiaeas, and *Scilla tubergeniana*. Try experimenting with other hardy bulbs as well.

Before a bulb is forced, the gardener must first choose the bulb, plant it and cool it. The key to each step lies in the timing.

Choosing Bulbs for Forcing. Whichever kind of bulb you choose, be sure the variety you purchase is marked "good for forcing," especially if—as is the case with tulips, hyacinths, and daffodils—many varieties are available. It is wise to order your selections well in advance—in the spring if possible—to ensure their availability. Most bulb suppliers will deliver at the right time for planting in your area.

If you receive an early shipment or for some reason can't plant the bulbs immediately, store them in a cool (35° to 50° F) place. The refrigerator is ideal, but don't put them in the same crisper as ripe fruit. If they are packed in boxes or paper bags, open them up to provide ventilation. Bulbs can be stored this way

Most bulbs are planted for forcing just as they are for other container growing. After these reticulata irises are planted, they will be covered with soil and watered.

Cooling bulbs in a trench. The trench will be filled with loose soil and mulched to keep the ground from freezing. This winter, the pots will be dug up a few at a time for forcing.

for several weeks. Remember that bulbs are living plants. Handle them carefully and avoid freezing them.

Planting. Bulbs can be planted during October or November to bloom from January through April. They require a cooling period of about 14 or 15 weeks. You can cool them for anywhere from 13 to 18 weeks, but the stems will be short on those cooled less than 14 weeks and long on those cooled more than 15 weeks.

In general, plant around the beginning of October for January flowers, the middle of October for February flowers, and the beginning and middle of November for March and April flowers.

The planting medium anchors the bulbs in place and holds moisture for rooting. Bulbs contain enough food for the developing flowers and shouldn't be fertilized during forcing. They must have excellent drainage or they will rot—but they shouldn't be allowed to dry out. Use clean pots that have drainage holes in the bottom. If you use clay pots, first soak them overnight so they won't draw moisture from the planting medium.

Fill each pot loosely with soil. The tops of the bulbs should be even with the rim when placed in the pot. Don't compress the soil or press the bulbs into it; the soil under the bulbs should remain loose so roots can grow through it easily. After the bulbs are in, fill the pots to the rim. The first watering will settle the soil enough to provide headspace for future watering.

Plant about 3 hyacinths, 6 daffodils or tulips, or 15 crocuses in a 6-inch pot or bulb pan. When planting tulips, place the bulb so that the flat side faces toward the outside of the pot. The first large leaf of each plant will then face outward, creating a uniform appearance. As you plant each pot, label it with the name of the variety, the planting date, and the date you intend to bring it indoors for forcing.

Cooling the Bulbs. All hardy bulbs need a period of cooling at temperatures between 35° and 50° F to prepare them for later leaf and flower growth.

Some bulbs, especially tulips that are sold in mild-climate regions, may have been partially "precooled" by the producer. These can be given the remainder of the 14 to 15 weeks of cold that they require, then planted for forcing. If you hold bulbs in the refrigerator for more than 3 weeks, subtract 3 weeks from the required cooling time.

Cooling methods vary, but any structure where temperatures can be kept at 35° to 50° F can be used. Many people find a root cellar or an unheated basement the most convenient; others use an old refrigerator. During this apparently inactive cooling period, the roots are forming, so the soil must be kept moist. Check the soil weekly.

In areas where the winter temperatures drop below zero, pots can be cooled in a trench in the garden or in a cold frame. With either of these methods, it is important to keep the pots from freezing. A frame used for this purpose should be shaded and well drained. After the pots are placed in the frame, cover them with insulating material, such as sand, sawdust, or straw.

If you choose to cool the bulbs in a trench, select a sloping location to aid in drainage. Dig a trench about 6 inches wider than the pots and deep enough for the pots to be below the frost line. Spread an inch of gravel or cinders on the bottom of the trench for drainage, and set the pots in the trench. Cover them with a few inches of sand, and finish filling the trench with soil.

Just before freezing weather, cover the trench with an insulating mulch. Bales of straw are convenient, and can be removed and replaced easily during the winter.

For a succession of blooms with either of these methods, place pots in storage in the reverse order in which you wish to remove them.

If there is any danger of mice burrowing into the mulch and damaging bulbs, top the trench with a ¼-inch-mesh wire screen before applying mulch. A diagram of where the pots are placed in the trench and which bulbs are in each will help you find what you want when you're ready to

force each pot indoors. If the weather is dry, water the pots frequently.

Forcing the Blooms. At the forcing stage, the pots are brought out of their cooled environment into warmth and light, triggering the formation of leaves and flowers. From the time the pots are removed from storage, they will require about three or four weeks to bloom. Bulbs planted on October 1 can be brought indoors around Christmas. Bring in a few pots every week after that for a continuous supply of blooms.

For best results, give the bulbs a temperature of 60° F and direct sunlight. Rotate the pots regularly so that all the leaves receive an equal amount of light. To prolong the bloom, remove the plants from direct sunlight when they begin to flower. Keep the soil moist throughout the forcing period.

If you're aiming for a specific flowering date and growth is occurring too quickly, blooming can be delayed by moving the pots to a cool (40° to 50° F) room out of direct sunlight (but not in darkness). Reaccustom them gradually to sunlight and warmer temperatures when you want them to resume growing.

After blooming, hardy bulbs cannot be forced again. A few, such as daffodils, can be transplanted into the garden in spring, but it will take them two or three years to reach their full blooming potential again. Most, such as tulips and hyacinths, are best discarded after forcing.

Soilless Forcing. Hyacinths are sometimes forced in special "hyacinth glasses," shaped like an hourglass, with an upper compartment for the bulb and a lower compartment into which the roots grow. The bottom of the bulb should be just at water level in the lower section of the glass. Add water as needed to maintain this level during growth. Cool the bulb in its con-

tainer for 14 to 15 weeks; then place it in bright light where daytime temperatures are 60° to 65° F. There are also tiny bottles in which crocuses can be grown the same way. This unusual method of forcing lets you watch the roots grow.

Forcing Without Cooling. The tender narcissus—paper-white (*Narcissus tazetta*), its yellow variety, 'Soleil d'Or', and large bulbs of the Chinese sacred lily (*Narcissus tazetta orientalis*)—can be forced without cooling. Successive plantings made about two weeks apart, from mid-October on, can give you indoor blooms from Thanksgiving until late March.

The usual—and very easy—way to grow them is to use an undrained, decorative bowl. First, fill the container with enough pebbles, gravel, coarse sand, pearl chips, or similar material to reach about 1 inch below the top. Add water until it is barely below the surface of the gravel. Set the bulbs on top and hold them in

This hyacinth glass makes a novel and attractive way to display a flowering bulb. The bulb is cooled and forced in the container, just as if it were in soil.

When you cut fresh flowers, small air bubbles are sometimes trapped in the end of the stem. These bubbles keep the bloom from absorbing water. To remove them, cut them a second time under water just before arranging.

These paper-white daffodils have been forced in a glass jar filled with pebbles. As in the hyacinth glass, the roots are visible and add interest to the flower.

place by adding enough gravel to cover the bottom quarter of the bulbs. Carefully maintain the water level.

An alternative method is to use vermiculite as a planting medium. Thoroughly saturate it; then gently squeeze out the excess moisture and place the vermiculite loosely in the container. Set the bulbs in place and partially cover them, leaving about three fourths of each bulb visible. The vermiculite should be kept evenly moist throughout the forcing process.

Tender narcissus are best kept in a cool (50° to 60° F) spot in low light until they are well-rooted and the shoots appear—usually about two to three weeks. They should then be placed in direct sunlight until they begin to flower, then moved into lower light. Because these bulbs cannot be forced again, after blooming they must be discarded.

Bulbs as Cut Flowers

Many bulbs produce long-lasting cut flowers. Select blooms that are just beginning to open, as well as a few buds that will open in a day or two. Gather flowers early or late in the day, but not in the heat of midday, when flowers contain the least water. Cut stems with clean, sharp scissors or a knife. Leave as much foliage on the plant as possible to store nutrients for the bulb. Carry a bucket of water with you to the garden and immediately plunge the flower stems into it. Don't combine tulips and daffodils in the same water; the sap of the daffodils will injure the tulips. If you wish to combine them in an arrangement, let each first sit in its own container of water for a few hours.

Removing flowers in most cases causes no harm to the plant and may even make it stronger the following year since the bulb will not have to exert energy for seed production.

If you don't wish to remove flowers from your landscape, consider planting a cutting garden of bulbs in an out-of-the-way area of your property, or plant a few rows of bulbs in the vegetable garden for cutting. By the time you need the space for tomatoes or squash, the bulbs will have ripened and been removed.

Another way to have fresh bulbs for cutting is to grow them very close together, in flats. The flats can be forced or allowed to bloom at their natural time, then discarded after cutting.

Florists use the following trick to keep long stems, such as those of tulips, straight. Lay a dozen or so of the stems on three or four thicknesses of newspaper and wrap them well. Tie the bundle together securely and stand it upright in tepid water almost reaching the lowest blossoms for a few hours or overnight. Recut stems underwater before putting them into a vase.

Commercially grown tulips to be shipped by air are first wrapped in plastic film or newspaper and then placed, under refrigeration, flat on a shelf for several days. When ready to be used, the flowers are given a fresh, sharp cut and plunged into tepid water. If you have a lot of tulips in the garden at one time and wish to store some for a while, you might try this idea. Tulips may also be stored upright with bulbs attached.

All cut stems should rest in tepid water almost to the lowest blossoms for several hours—

overnight, if possible. Recut the stems underwater with a clean, sharp knife before inserting them into the vase. These practices, together with clean vases and cutting tools and use of a floral preservative (or ¼ teaspoon liquid bleach and 1 teaspoon sugar per gallon of water), help keep the flowers fresh for as long as possible in the vase. Floral preservatives (or liquid bleach) prevent bacterial growth in the cut ends, which can impede water uptake. Sugar provides energy for the flower. Recutting the stems and changing the vase water daily (when feasible) also helps.

When you arrange the flowers, don't push tender, easily bruised stems into florist's foam, especially hollow stems such as those of narcissus. Poke a hole first with a pencil. Although most bulbs enjoy deep water, narcissus seem to last longer if the water level is kept shallow, just a few

inches at the bottom of the container. They drink a lot, so check the water level often.

Stems of tulips, anemones, ornithogalums, and a few other bulbs continue to grow in water, and it is difficult to keep them positioned properly in bouquets. Some people use florist's wire under the heads and through the stems, a practice that shortens their vase life. It probably makes more sense simply to turn them around or recut them when they go their own way.

Bulb flowers are beautiful displayed alone in bunches all of one kind or mixed or combined with foliage and other garden flowers. Even if you have no garden, a handful of fragrant freesias or narcissus, an extravagant bunch of irises, or a single gloriosa blossom from the florist can bring the fresh beauty of bulbs into your house in any season.

This flamboyant arrangement is made from spring bulbs. You can fill your house with fresh-cut flowers without stripping your landscape by planting some bulbs just for cutting. Grow them in an unused row in the vegetable garden, in an out-of-the-way cutting garden, or force them in flats.

Bulbs are so easy to raise that even beginners can create displays as beautiful as this window box full of 'Balalaika' tulips.

Raising the Strongest, Most Beautiful Bulbs

There are no secrets to raising strong, healthy bulbs, just a few simple principles based on the natural cycle of growth.

Bulbs come closer to guaranteeing success than any other type of garden plant. Since all the nutrients the flower needs are already stored in the bulb, it's hard to make a mistake. Probably the hardest part of raising a bulb is finding the one you want.

This chapter helps you with the task of selecting the bulbs you want to plant and finding where to buy them. You will find a list of sources for out-of-the-ordinary bulbs and information about various bulb societies, which can be a great aid in locating and growing bulbs. The discussions of planting and maintenance will help you naturalize your bulbs successfully, so that you will get blooms year after year.

What you read in this chapter applies to most bulbs (see the "Directory of Bulbs" for exceptions to these general rules), especially to the widely grown hardy bulbs. At the end of the chapter, you'll find descriptions of the common bulb pests and diseases, and instructions for preventing them.

Selecting Healthy Bulbs

Success begins with high-quality bulbs. Always buy from a reliable source, whether you are shopping at local outlets or ordering from catalogs. As with other goods, you're likely to get what you pay for. It's usually more economical in the long run to buy bulbs from a good source than to search out bargains.

Since the bulb stores the energy (in the form of starch) that makes the flower, larger bulbs mean more and larger flowers. That doesn't mean you should buy only the largest, highest-grade bulbs, however. Don't hesitate to buy lower-grade bulbs from reputable suppliers. These are simply smaller, less developed bulbs that need a season or so to catch up with bulbs of costlier grades. They are sensible purchases when you want large numbers of bulbs for naturalizing. Buy the largest (usually called *topsize*) bulbs when you want the most spectacular blooms this year.

When you buy bulbs locally, examine them closely. They should be firm and free from deep blemishes, cuts, or soft spots. They should feel heavy for their size, not light or dried up. It is very important that the basal plate of a true bulb (see page 8) be solid and firm. Small nicks and loose skin or tunics don't affect development. In fact, loose tunics help you spot harmful diseases.

Whether you purchase bulbs by mail or over the counter, plant them as soon as outdoor conditions are suitable. If planting must be delayed, store the bulbs in a cool place, such as a refrigerator. Do not store them in closed plastic bags—bulbs need to breathe. Open the plastic bags or transfer the bulbs into paper ones.

Topsize bulbs set close together in a pot make a stunning splash of color on a rainy spring afternoon. These are 'Delibes' daffodils.

Sources for Bulbs

The nurseries in this list vary from large commercial brokers to small, family-operated growers. But they all sell bulbs and bulb seeds by mail. A few are general plant and seed suppliers; these are included here because they publish a bulb catalog, usually in the fall. The rest specialize in bulbs—some in a single type of plant. A few British nurseries are also included because they carry some bulbs that are difficult to obtain in this country. Most of the nurseries charge for their catalogs, but many refund the purchase price with your first order. On requests for British price lists, enclose $3 to cover airmail costs.

Avon Bulbs
Bathford
Bath BA1 8ED
England
Exceptionally long list of bulbs.

B & D Lilies
330 P Street
Port Townsend, WA 98368
(206) 385-1738

Breck's Bulbs
6523 North Galena Road
Peoria, IL 61632
(309) 691-4616
Holland bulbs.

Burpee
300 Park Avenue
Warminster, PA 18991
(215) 674-4900, extension 222
Holland bulbs and lilies.
Request the bulb catalog.

P.J. and J.W. Christian
Pentre Cottages
Minera, Wrexham
Clwyd, N. Wales,
Great Britain
Many rare bulbs.

Cooley's Iris Gardens
Box 126
Silverton, OR 97381
Hybrid iris.

The Cottage Nursery
Potterton & Martin
Moortown Road, Mettleton
Caistor Lines LN7 6HX
England
Many rare bulbs.

C.A. Cruikshank
1015 Mt. Pleasant Road
Toronto, Ont. M4P 2M1
Canada
Wide variety.

Dutch Gardens, Inc.
Box 400
Montvale, NJ 07645
(201) 391-4366
Holland bulbs at wholesale rates.
$20 minimum.

Russell Graham
4030 Eagle Crest Road NW
Salem, OR 97304
(503) 362-1135
Species cyclamen and other bulbs.

Holbrook Farm & Nursery
Route 2, Box 223B
Fletcher, NC 28732
(404) 891-7790
Holland bulbs.

International Growers Exchange, Inc.
Box 52248
Livonia, MI 48152-0248
Very long list.

Jackson and Perkins
83-A Rose Lane
Medford, OR 97501
Holland bulbs.
Request a bulb catalog.

P. de Jager & Sons
Box 100
Brewster, NY 10509
(800) 343-1059
Holland bulbs and lilies.

McClure & Zimmerman
1422 West Thorndale
Chicago, IL 60660
(312) 989-0557
Long list of rare and unusual bulbs.

Messelaar Bulb Co.
150 County Road
Ipswich, MA 01938
(617) 356-3737
Holland bulbs.

Grant Mitsch Novelty Daffodils
Box 218
Hubbard, OR 97032
(503) 651-2742
Prolific hybridizers.

Oregon Bulb Farms
39391 S.E. Lusted Road
Sandy, OR 97053
(503) 663-3133
Lily breeders and growers. Also known as JAGRA and Jan de Graaff.

Park Seed Co.
Greenwood, SC 29647
(800) 845-3369
Holland bulbs.
Ask for their bulb catalog.

Quality Dutch Bulbs Inc.
Box 225
Hillsdale, NJ 07642
(201) 391-6586
Holland bulbs.

Rex Lilies
Box 774
Port Townsend, WA 98368
(206) 385-4280
Lilies only.

Royal Gardens
Box 588
Farmingdale, NJ 07727
Holland bulbs and lilies.

Mike Salmon
Jacklands Bridge
Tichenham, Nr. Clevedon
Avon BC21 6SQ
England
Some very rare bulbs.

John Scheepers, Inc.
63 Wall Street
New York, NY 10005
(212) 422-1177
Wide selection. Also publishes a "forcing edition" of bulbs.

Schreiners's Iris Garden
3625 Quinaby Road, NE
Salem, OR 97303
Hybrid iris.

Anthony Skittone
2271 31st Avenue
San Francisco, CA 94116
Wholesale rates, with $50 minimum. A very complete list.

C.F. and N.J. Stevens
40 Whittlesford Road
Newton, Cambridge, England
Long list.

Van Bourgondien Bros.
Box A, Route 109
Babylon, NY 11702
(516) 669-3500
Holland bulbs.

Vanderberg
Black Meadow Road
Chester, NY 10918
(800) 431-9003
All types of bulbs.

Wayside Gardens
Hodges, SC 29695
(800) 845-1124
Ask for the fall catalog.

White Flower Farm
Litchfield, CT 06759-0050
(203) 567-4565
Ask for the fall catalog.

Bulb Societies

As your interest in bulbs grows, you may find that you need further resources. Plant societies are associations of people with a common interest in some type of plant. Most publish a newsletter and loan books, and they are the best sources of information for individual plants.

American Begonia Society, Inc.
10331 S. Colim Road
Whittier, CA 90604
(213) 944-5641

American Daffodil Society
Route 3, 2302 Byhalia Road
Hernando, MS 38632
(601) 368-6337

American Dahlia Society
2044 Great Falls Street
Falls Church, VA 22043
(703) 532-8198

British Columbia Begonia and Fuchsia Society
2175 W. 16th Avenue
Vancouver, B.C. B6K 3B1
Canada

Canadian Gladiolus Society
1274-129A Street
Surrey, B.C. V4A 3Y4
Canada
(604) 536-8200

Canadian Iris Society
199 Florence Avenue
Willowdale, Ont. M2N 1G5
Canada
(416) 225-1088

Nerine Society
Brookend House
Welland, Worcestershire
England

North American Gladiolus Council
9338 Manzanita Drive
Sun City, AZ 84373
(602) 972-4177

North American Lily Society
Box 476
Waukee, IA 50263

Society for Louisiana Irises
Box 40175 USL
Lafayette, LA 70504
(318) 264-6203

The American Iris Society
7414 E. 60th Street
Tulsa, OK 74145
(918) 627-0706

Getting Ready

Choosing the right location for a bulb is vital to its success both in the garden and indoors. The first chapter talked about the types of climates to which bulbs are adapted. In the second chapter, you read about many ways of modifying the climate (with bulb frames and greenhouses) to grow bulbs that aren't adapted to your region. But your yard contains several—perhaps dozens—of different *microclimates*, such as under trees or against the south wall of your house.

As a gardener, you are probably already aware of the differences in the planting sites in your garden. When deciding where to place a new bulb, think of its needs and select a location that comes closest to giving it what it "expects." The level of light can vary dramatically within just a few feet—from the edge of a shrub to the corner of your house. The sunlight reflected from a south-facing wall or fence can create conditions that will help a bulb adapted to the hot, dry summers of a Mediterranean climate. A bulb adapted to woodlands will appreciate a site where it receives morning sun but is shielded from the afternoon sun. Microclimates in your garden will support bulbs from many different climates.

Preparing the Soil. Most bulbs adapt to many types of soil, but nearly all prefer a loose, porous soil structure. With only a few exceptions—such as Siberian irises, which tolerate swampy conditions—bulbs must have good drainage. If your soil doesn't drain quickly, improve the drainage by adding soil amendments, planting in raised beds, or installing drain lines to carry away excess water.

Before planting, prepare the soil so that the roots can move through it easily and water will drain through quickly. Both heavy clay soils and extremely sandy soils can be improved by adding an organic amendment,

Every garden is composed of a multitude of microclimates, some as small as a space between two rocks. The rocks store heat and protect these 'King Alfred' daffodils from the weather.

such as compost, humus, ground and composted bark, or peat moss. In heavier soils, organic material separates the soil particles, letting water and air move more easily through the soil. Organic matter incorporated into sandy soils acts like a sponge, holding more moisture and nutrients for the plants.

In fact, organic matter will improve almost any soil. Add the amendment you select by spreading it over the surface of the area you intend to plant. Spread the amendment at least 1 inch—but not more than 4 inches—deep and work it into the soil.

Fertilizing. When you plant, mix some bone meal or superphosphate into the soil at the bottom of each planting hole. Phosphorus, supplied by both of these fertilizers, must be present deep in the soil, where the bulb roots are. Phosphorus does not move readily through the soil as other plant nutrients do, so it must be placed at a depth where the roots can reach it.

Fertilize again when foliage begins to emerge, usually in the spring. Spread a fertilizer containing nitrogen and potash on the ground around the plants and wash it into the soil with a thorough irrigation. The fertilizer label will tell you how much to use.

For summer- and fall-blooming bulbs that need fertilizing, apply half the amount of fertilizer recommended on the label every month until the foliage begins to yellow. If the bulb is evergreen, continue the feeding program until fall; then begin again when growth resumes in spring.

Some bulbs, such as belladonna lilies and colchicum, bloom after the foliage has died. Feed them only when, before, and during the time they are in leaf, not when they are blooming.

Planting

As a rule, plant bulbs as soon as possible after receiving them. This prevents them from drying out. Lilies are especially delicate and should go into the ground immediately. If you live in a warm climate, delay planting early-spring bulbs by keeping them refrigerated or stored in a cool place until warm weather is past, to avoid premature sprouting and damage from winter cold.

Most bulbs are planted at a depth that is equal to three times their diameter. Check the "Directory of Bulbs" for specific depths. When you plant several bulbs close together, it is easier to dig up the entire area to the proper depth, set the bulbs in the hole, and cover them. When planting smaller numbers, and especially in crowded areas among other plants, dig individual holes with a bulb planter or a trowel. Place the bulb in the hole, cover it with soil, and firm the soil slightly with your hands.

Planting in Containers. Quick drainage is even more important for bulbs in containers than it is for those in the ground. Make a soil-based mix of equal parts garden loam, coarse sand, and organic matter such as peat moss or ground bark; or plant in a packaged mix. Some bulbs—see the "Directory of Bulbs"—require the addition of dolomitic limestone at a rate of between 3 to 5 ounces for each bushel of growing medium.

Shallow (4 to 5 inches deep) clay pots known as *bulb pans* are an attractive, useful choice for many bulbs, although hippeastrum, lily, and other large bulbs, as well as some smaller, deep-growing ones such as fritillaria, need regular pots. Shallow barrels, ceramic planters, plastic pots, and a host of other typical garden containers work satisfactorily.

Cover the drainage holes with pieces of window screen or potsherds, add soil, and position the bulbs, setting them closer together than you would in the ground. See the "Directory of Bulbs" for the best spacing or number of bulbs per pot. Most pots of flowers look best if the bulbs are almost touching. Plant each tulip bulb with the flat side facing the edge of the pot. Large bulbs such as hippeastrum and lily are best planted individually in 6- to 8-inch pots.

If the containers will be protected during winter or if you are planting in the spring after frost danger, set the bulbs with their tips just under the soil surface, instead of at the depth suggested for garden planting. Fill the pot to the rim with loose soil. The first watering will settle the soil enough to make headspace for future waterings. Soak the soil thoroughly after planting and place the pots in a cool area until the bulbs root.

If the potted bulbs are to be forced, store or bury them as instructed on page 21. If the bulbs are to be grown as greenhouse specimens or houseplants, place them where their light and heat requirements can be met after the shoots emerge.

If bulbs are to be grown outdoors in cold climates, plant them at the same time that you would plant them in the ground. Protect fall-planted container bulbs by placing them in a frame, or bury them in a trench as for forcing, leaving them covered until frost danger is past. Treat spring-planted container bulbs as you would if they were planted in the ground.

Keep container-planted bulbs evenly moist throughout their growing and blooming period. Then reduce watering as bulbs begin their rest period, signaled by yellowing leaves.

Watering

Unless the ground is rain soaked, water thoroughly after planting bulbs. Winter or spring rains usually provide the rest of the moisture needed until the bulbs sprout. But if you live in a climate with dry periods during the winter, you may need to water again. Don't let the soil dry out.

When the plants are a few inches tall, begin watering to keep them evenly moist throughout the growing and blooming period. Bulb roots grow deep; watering should be thorough, not just a surface sprinkling. The amount of water, of course, depends on the weather and the rate of growth. Bulbs need regular watering during active growth, which includes the period of root development before sprouting starts. Continue to water after the blooms fade, until the foliage turns yellow.

Maintaining Planted Areas. Although it's not good for all bulbs in all seasons, mulching with organic material helps the bulbs in several important ways. It discourages weeds. In cold-winter areas it insulates against cold and helps prevent damage caused by alternating freezing and thawing of the ground and by late frosts. In summer, particularly in dry climates, it not only keeps soil temperatures down but also slows drying out—advantages for some bulbs, disadvantages for others. It can deflect rain or sprinkler water—again, to the advantage of some bulbs and the detriment of others. Some tender or semi-hardy bulbs that benefit from a dry baking in summer also benefit from insulation against cold in winter, so they should be mulched seasonally, not the year around. On page 15 read about mulching rock-garden areas with gravel.

To keep bulb plants looking neat, remove the spent flowers with scissors or a sharp knife, cutting just below the bloom and leaving the stem on the plant. This does no harm to the bulbs and channels energy into the bulb instead of seed production. However, the leaves must be allowed to remain long enough to store energy for next year's flowers. Don't cut or pull them off unless you plan to discard the bulbs after blooming. It's best to let the foliage remain until it has turned yellow. If you can't stand its messy appearance, leave it for at least six weeks.

Foliage hidden by a ground cover, such as pachysandra or vinca, or by perennials in a border won't need any special attention. You can also hide yellowing foliage with annuals, but be careful not to damage the bulbs as you plant them.

Lifting and Storing

At the onset of their dormancy, many bulbs require drying off (see page 6), and tender bulbs require protection from cold. In wet-summer or cold-winter areas, the bulbs must be dug and stored. Some container-grown bulbs may be moved to sheltered areas in their containers, but others do better if they are removed from the soil. A spading fork is the least likely of the digging tools to slice bulbs—but when there are casualties, discard them. Shake the dug bulbs free of soil and dry them for a few days in a shady, well-ventilated spot. Dust them with a fungicide or a commercial bulb dust to prevent rotting in storage. If the bulb is prone to an insect

problem—such as thrips on gladiolus—add an insecticide.

Different bulbs have different storage requirements; see the "Directory of Bulbs." Some bulbs are stored in open air, others in a packing medium such as sand, vermiculite, or peat moss. Usually the medium must be dry, although some bulbs require slight moisture. Some bulbs require cool storage conditions (35° to 55° F), some warm (60° to 75° F). Some summer-dormant bulbs require storage, undug, in direct sun and heat. Unless the "Directory of Bulbs" indicates otherwise, assume that a winter-dormant bulb prefers cool, dry storage in a packing medium.

Propagation

Most gardeners know the arithmetic of basic gardening—how to multiply by dividing. Most of the bulbs mentioned in this book can be multiplied (propagated) by dividing their tuberous roots, tubers, or rhizomes or by

separating new corms and bulbs from the original. In some cases—tulips, for instance—the old bulb disappears, leaving behind one or more offspring.

Nearly all bulbous plants may also be propagated from seeds. Though bulbs grown from seeds sometimes take several years to flower, seeding has a number of advantages. Some species are most widely available as seeds. Seeds are less expensive than bulbs. Seeds offer the possibility of varied flower forms and colors because of genetic variation. This opens the wide door of hybridizing, with all its attendant excitement. As gardeners become more and more interested in a particular plant, they often want to improve it.

Another gratification derives from knowing that you haven't risked purchasing bulbs taken from the wild, particularly if a species is rare and endangered. For most popular garden bulbs, seeds often aren't available; for other bulbs, however, seeding is a sound and useful method of propagation.

These lily bulbs are being stored in a plastic food bag, packed in peat moss. Since bulbs need to breathe in storage, slits were first cut in the bag to allow ventilation. The peat moss will keep the bulbs at just the right moisture content. Paper and net bags also store bulbs well, as do planting flats.

Propagation Techniques

Here are nine of the most useful propagation techniques that are used with bulbs. The "Directory of Bulbs" tells you which methods work best with each bulb.

Scoring. This propagation method is commonly used on hyacinths but also works on narcissus and scilla. Make three cuts through the basal plate in early summer. Store in a dry spot for a few days until the cuts open. Dust the cut surfaces with captan, and place the bulbs in a warm, dark place with high humidity for a few months. After bulblets have formed in the fall, plant the mother bulb upside down in the garden. The bulblets will sprout in the spring.

Seeding. Most bulbs can be started from seeds. To start most kinds of seeds outdoors, plant them (unless otherwise indicated in the "Directory of Bulbs") so they are just barely covered by soil. Keep the soil moist but not wet until the seeds germinate, then let it dry slightly between waterings. To start seeds indoors, plant them in damp vermiculite in pots or flats. If the seeds are very fine, don't cover them with soil. Cover the flat or pot with plastic film and keep it in a warm place. As soon as the seedlings are large enough to handle, transplant them to pots. Generally, summer growers require warmth to germinate and should be sown in the spring. Winter growers, however, need cool or cold conditions to ensure later germination, so they should be sown in the fall, or stratified—refrigerated in a moist medium—to break dormancy before sowing.

Scaling. This method is used to propagate lilies and other scaly bulbs. Break or cut the scales close to the basal plate. You can remove the two outer rows of scales without damaging a large bulb. Dust the scales with captan and a rooting powder, then seal them in a plastic bag with damp vermiculite. Keep the bag at room temperature until bulblets form— about two months—and cool it in a refrigerator for another two months to overcome dormancy. Then plant the new bulblets.

Dividing Rhizomes. Lift the rhizomes of flowers such as bearded irises after flowering. Discard old rhizomes (those without leaves) and cut the remainder into sections, leaving one fan of leaves on each section. Trim both the leaves and the roots to about 3 inches. Replant immediately just under the surface of the soil.

Bulb Cuttings. Propagate narcissus, hippeastrum, and other tunicate bulbs by this method. Cut a mature bulb into eight sections vertically, then slip a knife between the scales and cut the basal plate so that there are four scale segments on each piece of basal plate. Plant these cuttings in vermiculite with the tips of the segments just above the surface. Treat these cuttings like stem cuttings, directions for which are given to the right. New bulblets will form between the scales in a few weeks.

Rooting Stem Cuttings. Cut dahlia stems when they are about 4 inches high. Take a piece of the crown with the cutting. Place the cutting in a pot of damp vermiculite and cover with a plastic bag held away from the cutting with a loop of wire. Fasten the bag with a rubber band. Place the pot in a warm bright spot but not in direct sun. Water as necessary by placing the pot in a pan of water for 10 minutes. Roots will form in a couple of weeks. Transplant to a soil mix when the new roots begin to branch.

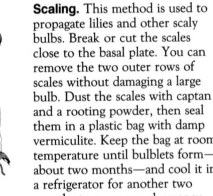

Dividing Tuberous Roots. After the eyes have begun to swell in the spring and are clearly visible, divide tuberous roots into segments. Each segment must have at least one eye. Dust the cut surface with captan and cure in a dry, warm place for two days. Plant in the garden with the eyes about 2 inches deep.

Propagating With Cormels. These tiny corms are offsets formed around the edges of large corms. The shallower a corm is planted, the more cormels it will form. Store cormels in slightly damp peat moss over the winter, and plant them about 2 inches deep in the spring. A few might reach flowering size the first year, but most will need a second year of growth.

Propagating With Bulblets and Bulbils. Some species of lilies form tiny, globular bulbils at the base of the leaves. So do some tulips and alliums. Some lily species can be induced to form clusters of bulbils by disbudding the mother plant and mounding soil around the stem or bending and burying its lower two thirds in a shallow trench. Bulbils will form along the buried portion over the summer. Many true bulbs form tiny offsets called bulblets around the parent bulb. Separate and plant bulblets in fall and bulbils as soon as they are ripe. Plant both the bulblets and bulbils 1 to 2 inches deep.

Controlling Bulb Pests And Diseases

The most common pests and diseases of bulbs are described here. For further information about bulb problems, contact your county extension agent. You can prevent many problems by good garden practices:
• Keep the garden clean and free of weeds.
• Give bulbs the soil, water, and exposure they need.
• Keep a sharp watch for signs of pests or for diseased leaves or flowers, and deal with the problem promptly.

Aphids
Common hosts: Anemone, begonia, dahlia, gladiolus, hyacinth, iris, lily, tulip.
Damage: Curled or twisted leaves; yellowing of foliage.
Control: Spray with malathion, diazinon, carbaryl, or acephate.

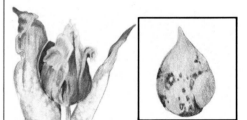

Botrytis
Common hosts: Tuberous begonia, dahlia, hyacinth, daffodil, gladiolus, lily, tulip.
Damage: Spotted, then blighted leaves and flowers; slimy, collapsed leaves or flowers; gray, fuzzy mold on plant.
Control: Pick up old leaves and flowers; plant bulbs in areas with good air circulation; apply captan to soil and bulbs before planting. Spray with benomyl.

Fungus diseases (various)
Common hosts: most bulbs.
Damage: Stunted yellow growth; mushy or dried-out bulbs.
Control: Handle bulbs carefully when planting or digging to avoid damaging surface; discard rotted bulbs; treat bulbs with fungicide before planting or storing.

Japanese beetles
Common hosts: Canna, dahlia.
Damage: Chewed holes in stems, leaves, or flowers.
Control: Spray with malathion, carbaryl, or diazinon.

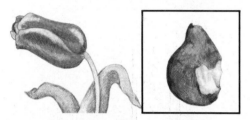 

Gophers, voles, and other ground-dwelling animals
Common hosts: Tulip, crocus, and many others.
Damage: Eaten bulbs.
Control: Plant in raised beds or containers; set traps; use poisoned bait; plant in underground "baskets" made of 1-inch or smaller wire mesh.

Mites
Common hosts: Amaryllis, begonia, crocus, cyclamen, freesia, gladiolus, hyacinth, lily, daffodil, tulip.
Damage: Finely stippled, pale leaves; lack of growth.
Control: Hose down plants regularly in dry weather; destroy badly infested bulbs; spray plants with dicofol.

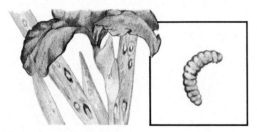 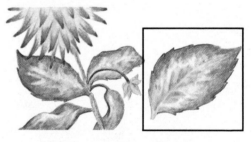

Iris borer
Common host: Iris.
Damage: Tunneling through leaves, boring into rhizomes, causing rot.
Control: Spray weekly with malathion during April and May.

Mosaic or yellows diseases
Common hosts: Canna, crocus, dahlia, gladiolus, hyacinth, iris, lily, daffodil, scilla, zantedeschia.
Damage: Mottled or yellow leaves, distorted foliage or flowers, stunted growth.
Control: Destroy infected plants; destroy disease-spreading aphids.

Narcissus fly larvae

Common hosts: Amaryllis, galanthus, hymenocallis, leucojum, narcissus, zephranthes.
Damage: Eaten bulb centers; yellow, deformed leaves; stunted growth.
Control: Discard soft bulbs. Dust soil or bulbs with diazinon; sprinkle soil around plants with naphthalene.

Slugs and snails

Common hosts: Agapanthus, canna, dahlia, lily, tulip.
Damage: Holes in leaves, eaten young shoots, slime trails.
Control: Remove all debris; put out snail bait when first shoots emerge.

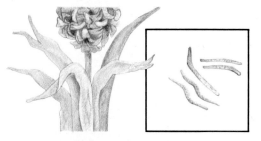

Nematodes

Common hosts: Dahlia, galanthus, gladiolus, hyacinth, iris, lily, lycoris, daffodil, tigridia.
Damage: Deformed or split leaves; yellow and brown blotches on foliage; browned bulb tissue.
Control: Destroy infested plants and bulbs; fumigate soil (consult local nursery, garden center or agricultural extension office).

Thrips

Common hosts: Allium, amaryllis, begonia, dahlia, freesia, gladiolus, lily, sinningia.
Damage: Streaks of gray or brown on foliage or flowers, sticky brown surface on stored bulbs.
Control: Spray growing plants with malathion or acephate (check labels); dust bulbs with diazinon before storing.

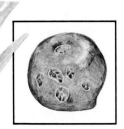

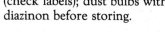

Scab

Common host: Gladiolus.
Damage: Lesions on corms, spotted leaves.
Control: Dust corms with captan; discard infested corms.

Wireworms

Common hosts: Begonia, dahlia, gladiolus.
Damage: Eaten-through stems causing plants to collapse.
Control: Treat bulbs and soil with diazinon before planting.

Lily-of-the-valley
*(Convallaria
majalis)* is one of
the most beloved
flowers in colder
parts of the coun-
try. It makes a
beautiful ground
cover or pot plant
and blends into any
woodland setting.
This variety is
'Rosea'.

Directory of Bulbs

An introduction to the diversity of flowering bulbs, from the hardy spring tulips and daffodils to the tender achimenes and the fall-blooming colchicums.

Throughout the remainder of this book you will find an array of bulbs, ranging from widely grown old favorites to intriguing exotics that are just beginning to find their way into horticulture in this country. Many are available in almost all local garden centers during their planting season. Others are difficult to locate; as an aid, see the list of nurseries on page 26. If you're really stumped, contact a plant society. For a list of plant societies primarily concerned with bulbs, see page 27.

Entries are alphabetized by the botanical name of the genus. Some plants are occasionally sold by an older, superseded botanical name. In these cases, the *synonym* (as superseded names are called) appears in parentheses immediately below the botanical name. When there are one or more widely accepted common names, they follow the botanical name. Many bulbs are popularly known by their botanical names—for example, gladiolus and iris. Throughout the text we use botanical names as common names to refer to bulbs that have no generally accepted common name—for example, geissorhiza and ixia.

Because common names aren't standardized, their use can result in confusion; for example, two entirely different bulbs are commonly called spider lily, and amaryllis is the botanical name but not the common name of one plant and the common name but not the botanical name of another.

The small maps show where the bulb is adapted. The dark blue portion of the map shows the areas where the plant can be naturalized with normal garden care. For some houseplants, this may be only a small area in the southern tip of Florida. The light blue portion shows the areas where the bulb can be grown outdoors with some special precautions, such as lifting the bulb and storing it during the winter. The uncolored portion shows areas where the plant is very difficult to grow as a perennial plant. However, it can still be grown in these areas in bulb frames or greenhouses. Of course, some bulbs can be grown indoors in all parts of the country, and many can be grown as annuals in any part of the country, then discarded after blooming.

The adaptation maps indicate how much trouble it might be to raise a given plant in your part of the country, not whether you should try to raise it; if your heart is set on a certain plant, by all means give it a try. By following the directions given earlier, you can succeed with bulbs in parts of the country to which they are not normally adapted. For many of the less-popular bulbs described in this book, there is little information about their adaptation in this country, and the maps are based on educated guesses, not experience. Part of the fun of gardening is experimenting with new plants and breaking the generally accepted rules about where plants will grow. Try any bulbs that appeal to you. If you find our map to be wrong, let us know; we will correct the map in the next edition, and you will have helped to expand the frontiers of gardening knowledge.

This is *Triteleia laxa.* It is sometimes sold by its older botanical name of *Brodiaea laxa.* In different parts of the country, it is known as Ithuriel's spear, ground nut, and triplet lily.

Following the name of a bulb are these facts: The family name, the category of the bulb (true bulb, corm, tuber, tuberous root, or rhizome), whether it is deciduous or evergreen, and its blooming season in the garden. Of course its blooming season will be different indoors.

A summary of cultural information is divided into four headings.

Location: Tells you where you can grow the bulb best. *Container* refers to a pot or other container kept outdoors; *house, greenhouse,* and *alpine house* (in most cases) indicate container culture in some type of sheltered situation. *Alpine house* refers not just to an alpine house, but also to a bulb frame or a cool, well-ventilated greenhouse, all of which offer the growing conditions discussed on page 17. Outdoor locations are for the parts of the country where the plant is adapted to outdoor growth. Information in the text of each entry will help you decide whether a bulb is adapted to your outdoor climate.

Soil: Gives soil requirements. Many bulbs can tolerate a wide range of soil acidity or alkalinity as long as it isn't too extreme.

Care: Gives watering and fertilizing requirements during different periods of growth and dormancy. If a bulb requires special treatment during dormancy, you will find instructions here or in the text.

Exposure: Tells you the amount of light a bulb needs or can tolerate.

In the text of each entry, you will find information about the bulb's origin, which will help you to understand what conditions the bulb "expects" in the garden or home. You will also find a physical description, some suggestions for using the bulb in the garden or house, and its availability.

You will also find information on planting and care to augment the general information given earlier in the book—when to plant, how deep, how far apart to put the bulbs in the ground or in a pot, what propagation methods work best, and which diseases and pests pose major threats.

Although we occasionally mention that a plant is poisonous, this shouldn't deter you from planting it. Many common garden plants are toxic if eaten. Avoid toxic plants if a small child or pet in your family is in the habit of chewing on leaves or berries, but they are safe to grow—and even to use in table decorations—if they aren't eaten.

Achimenes hybrid 'Valse Blue'

Achimenes

Orchid pansy, Mother's Tears

Gesneria family.
Scaly rhizome; deciduous.
Blooms late spring to fall.

Location: Greenhouse, house, lath house, or shaded bed outdoors.

Soil: Light, organic, neutral to slightly acid; commercial African violet mix is appropriate, or equal parts peat moss, perlite, and leaf mold.

Care: Water and feed constantly during period of growth and blooming, using 5-10-5 fertilizer; then gradually dry out at 50° to 60° F in fall, and keep dry until spring.

Exposure: Partial to full shade outdoors, moderate light indoors.

Neither orchid nor pansy despite its common name, this genus from Central and South America is related to African violets and gloxinias and has many of the same cultural needs. A well-grown specimen of a typical hybrid outshines its cousins—with dark, fuzzy leaves hidden by a solid mass of blossoms in a 6- to 18-inch mound for 2 months or longer. (However, some achimenes are upright rather than mounding.) A typical blossom is 2 to 2½ inches wide, and some are as wide as 3 inches. Colors range from white to lilac,

Achimenes andersonii

purple, scarlet, cerise, pink, salmon, and yellow. Some flowers are delicately veined. Its mounding, sometimes cascading, habit makes achimenes suitable for hanging baskets, though it is also at home in pots and in summer garden beds in warm humid areas. Specialists and some general suppliers sell it.

In early spring plant the rhizomes 1 inch deep and at least 2 inches apart, or five or six per 6-inch pot. For color over several months, stagger plantings from early spring to early summer. In the early stages of growth, pinch the shoot tips to encourage a lush, compact habit. Achimenes prefers a cool, dry place with 50° to 60° F temperatures. At the end of the season, after drying, the rhizomes can either be dug and stored, or left in pots, unwatered, in a warm, humid spot.

Propagate by dividing the rhizomes when you repot, rooting stems or leaves (this works for some varieties) in a peat-and-sand mixture. The powderlike seeds can be germinated by sowing them on the surface of moist soil in a container covered by glass or clear plastic and kept at 70° to 80° F, then at 70° F after germination.

Acidanthera bicolor

(*A. murieliae*)
See *Gladiolus callianthus*, page 67.

Agapanthus africanus

Agapanthus

Lily-of-the-Nile, African lily

Allium family.
Rhizomatus tuber; evergreen or
deciduous.
Blooms late spring to early fall.

Location: Greenhouse, house,
border.

Soil: Any with reasonable drainage,
though rich, slightly acid soil produces best results.

Care: Tolerates dryness but thrives
with regular watering and feeding
during period of growth, light watering and no feeding in winter.

Exposure: Partial shade in hot climates, full sun or partial shade
elsewhere.

Imposing with
its many dense
umbels of blos-
soms on long
stems, this easy-to-
grow South African pro-
duces large clumps of glossy,
straplike, evergreen leaves that are
decorative even when the plant is out
of flower. The several widely available cultivars, whose species names
(A. africanus, A. orientalis,
A. umbellatus) are frequently
confused in the trade, range in height
from 1 to 5 feet and in flower color
from white to light or dark blue.
'Peter Pan' and 'Queen Anne', blue-
flowered varieties under 2 feet tall,
are vigorous growers and reliable
bloomers. Most agapanthus are evergreen in mild-winter climates. The
scale of the larger forms suits them to
big pots or tubs, in which they are
graceful landscape or patio features
and can be moved to frost-free spots
during the winter. Where temperatures do not drop below 20° F, agapanthus can be planted one inch
deep and used to fill large areas, even
in fairly heavy shade (though blooms
will be sparse there).

A very satisfactory cut flower, agapanthus lasts five to seven days in a
vase. Seed heads may be air dried for
dried arrangements.

Allow plants to become root-
bound in containers before dividing—usually in four or five years—
because roots do not like to be disturbed. Seeds are easy to start at
about 75° F; seedlings bloom after
three to five years. With deep planting and mulching, roots may survive
winters in some areas outside the
usual climate range.

*Agapanthus
africanus*

*Albuca
candide*

Albuca canadensis

Albuca

Lily family.
True bulb; deciduous.
Blooms winter, late spring, or early
summer.

Location: Border, rock garden, container, alpine house.

Soil: Well drained, sandy, organic,
acid to neutral.

Care: Water regularly during period
of growth and blooming, late fall to
early summer; then reduce watering
or dry off until late fall. No fertilizing
is necessary in most garden soils.

Exposure: Sun.

Subtle rather
than showy
beauty, easy cul-
ture, and useful-
ness as a long-
lasting cut flower are

assets of this African-lily relative.
The whitish petals usually have a
green vein running down the center.
Albuca is hardy to 20° F.

In early fall plant bulbs 2 to 5
inches deep and 12 inches apart in
the garden, or 2 inches deep in a pot,
with three bulbs per 6-inch pot. Water initially, wait about a month for
growth to commence, then begin regular watering. Albuca is usually dried
off at the end of its season but tolerates summer rain if drainage is rapid.
Propagate it from offsets in early fall.

These two species are available
from specialists.

A. canadensis, forms of which are
sold as *A. major* and *A. minor,* grows
up to 3 feet and has nodding yellow
or greenish yellow flowers.

A. nelsonii has fragrant, nodding
white flowers, striped red, on stems
to 5 feet tall.

Occasionally you may also find
summer-growing *A. humilis,* a 4-inch
dwarf for rock gardens, containers,
or alpine house.

Allium neopolitanum

Allium

Ornamental onion

Allium family.
True bulbs; deciduous.
Bloom time varies by species, late spring or summer.

Location: Rock garden, border, woodland, meadow, container, house, greenhouse.

Soil: Most well-drained soils, though sandy, not-too-rich; acid-to-neutral soil is generally best.

Care: Most thrive on regular watering during the growing period and little or no feeding. Where they are not hardy, the bulbs should be dried off and stored over winter.

Exposure: Sun or light shade, unless otherwise noted below.

Native to various places in the Northern Hemisphere, this large, diverse group of ornamental cousins of onions, garlic, chives, and shallots has a wide range of uses for home gardeners in much of the country. Most smaller species are assets to rock gardens or container plantings indoors or out. Larger alliums provide a long season of summer color for borders. Some alliums are suited to woodland culture.

Allium giganteum

Alliums bear clusters of flowers atop straight, leafless stems; clusters are spherical, and, depending on the species, may be either loose or tight, or sparse or dense. Some alliums are among the best cut flowers, lasting as long as three weeks. A few are delightfully fragrant. The leaves of only a few smell like onions—and most of those only when they are bruised. Alliums make excellent dried flowers. Most species listed here are readily available from general suppliers and specialists.

Plant in the fall, 4 or 5 inches deep for most, deeper for larger bulbs. Leave them in place so plants can clump or reseed. Some species (but not those included here, except for A. *triquetrum* and A. *unifolium*) can become invasive. Divide only when containers or planting spaces become too crowded. Propagate in the fall by division or by seeds sown outdoors, or indoors after they have been refrigerated for four weeks in a moist medium.

A. *aflatunense* grows 2 to 5 feet tall and produces dense, spherical, 2- to 3-inch spheres of purple flowers in late spring. It is similar to A. *giganteum* but smaller.

A. *caeruleum* (A. *azureum*) grows 1 to 2½ feet tall and has dense umbels, 1 to 1½ inches wide, of bright sky-blue, in late spring and early summer.

A. *christophii* (A. *albopilosum*), called 'Star of Persia', produces 6- to 10-inch-wide umbels of silvery purple flowers on 1- to 2-foot stems in late spring. They are excellent for dried arrangements. Bulbs require drying off during summer dormancy.

A. *flavum* is perfectly suited to rock garden and container culture, especially its dwarf forms 'Nassum' and 'Minor'. Flowers are yellow and appear in late spring.

A. *giganteum* (giant allium) is well named. It carries its 5- to 6-inch spherical umbels of purple flowers atop stems 3 to 6 feet tall, in early or midsummer. It is a useful border plant. Plant bulbs 8 inches deep and 12 inches apart.

A. *karataviense* produces 4- to 5-inch umbels of lilac to pink flowers on stems only 7 or 8 inches tall. It blooms in late spring and is perfect for rock gardens and containers.

A. *moly* (lily leek) is similar to dwarf forms of A. *flavum* but is more readily available. It naturalizes easily and is suitable for rock gardens, borders, and containers. It bears loose umbels of small yellow flowers on 10- to 15-inch stems in late spring. Because of its oniony smell, it is not suitable for cutting.

A. *narcissiflorum*, a clumping, rhizomatous species from the Alps, is especially suited to containers and rock gardens. It is 6 to 12 inches high and has sparse-flowered umbels of graceful, bell-shaped white or pink to wine-colored flowers in summer.

A. *neopolitanum* 'Grandiflorum' is suitable for rock gardens and borders and naturalizes readily—too readily, in some gardeners' views. Its 12- to 18-inch stems bear sweet white flowers in loose 2-to 4-inch umbels in the spring or early summer. It is an excellent cut flower.

A. *sphaerocephalum* (drumsticks) is useful for naturalizing in lightly shaded woodland gardens and borders. In early summer it bears oblong clusters of reddish purple flowers on 1- to 2-foot stems. It is excellent for cutting and for drying.

A. *triquetrum*, in late spring and early summer bears loose umbels of bell-like white flowers striped with green, on stems up to 1½ feet tall above ground-hugging foliage. It prefers semishaded places. Where adapted, it can be invasive.

A. *unifolium*, native to the moist meadows of California, grows to 2 feet tall and in mid- or late spring bears bright rose-pink flowers in open umbels. Grow it in any sunny, moist or dry spot. Where adapted, it can become invasive.

Alstroemeria ligtu

Amaryllis belladonna

Alstroemeria

Peruvian lily, Lily-of-the-Incas

Alstroemeria family.
Tuberous roots.
Blooms late spring to early or mid-summer, one species in late summer and fall.

Location: Meadow, border, container, greenhouse.

Soil: Cool, well drained, acid to neutral.

Care: Water generously; feed periodically in spring until flowering ends, then water infrequently and stop feeding.

Exposure: Partial shade in hot climates, full sun elsewhere.

So spectacular is the blazing display of a large planting of alstroemeria at the University of California Botanical Garden, Berkeley, that an annual festival celebrates it. Most varieties and hybrids of these Chilean, Peruvian, or Brazilian natives are hardy where temperatures drop to 0° F if planted deep—about 8 inches—and mulched in winter; in colder areas roots can be dug and stored at about 40° F in damp sand, though often the plants don't survive digging. Where well adapted, some alstroemerias—notably *A. aurantiaca*—naturalize and become invasive. Azalea-like 2-inch flowers, borne in clusters atop erect, lilylike stems 3 or 4 feet tall in most species, are etched, blotched, and often bicolored. Colors range from tints of warm yellow, orange, gold, apricot,

pink, salmon, and red to cool mauve, purple, lavender, cream, and white.

Because of its long-stemmed gracefulness, attractive foliage, brilliant flowers, and long vase life (usually two weeks), alstroemeria is one of the best cut flowers, and is becoming increasingly available in florist shops.

In fall or early spring, plant the tuberous roots at least 6 inches deep and 1 foot apart, spreading out roots and taking care not to break them. Division often kills the plants. Alstroemeria can also be propagated from fresh seeds sown outdoors in early spring or indoors with a soil temperature of 55° F. Alstroemerias are sold by specialists and occasionally by some general suppliers.

A. aurantiaca, bright orange or yellow with contrasting markings, grows to 3 or 4 feet. The several named varieties and hybrids are all quite hardy. This species can be dug with less risk than the others.

A. ligtu and its hybrids are 3 to 4 feet tall, with flowers ranging from white to pink, salmon, and orange and beautifully marked and shaded. Like *A. aurantiaca*, this group is available from specialists and a few general nurseries.

Dr. Salter's hybrids, nearly 4 feet tall, bloom just a bit earlier than the Ligtu hybrids and are generally brighter colored.

Less available and less hardy (to 10° F) is *A. pulchella*, from Brazil, with scarlet flowers flecked with brown and tipped with greenish gold. Unlike the others, this one flowers in late summer and fall.

Amaryllis belladonna

Belladonna lily, Naked Lady

Amaryllis family.
True bulb; deciduous.
Blooms late summer or fall.

Location: Meadow, border, container.

Soil: Most soils with reasonable drainage.

Care: Water regularly only during period of active growth. Give complete fertilizer in late summer.

Exposure: Full sun in the hottest spot in the garden.

Not to be confused with its showy tropical American cousin hippeastrum (commonly called amaryllis and popular as a houseplant), the South African belladonna lily has extraordinary beauty of its own. The sudden emergence, after foliage has died, of 2- to 3-foot reddish stalks topped by clusters of 4- to 6-inch pink, rosy red, or white blossoms lends drama and color to the late-season garden in regions where the temperature doesn't drop below –10° F.

The strongly scented belladonna lily is an excellent cut flower, lasting for about a week.

Bulbs are available from specialists in late spring or early summer during dormancy and should be planted 2 to 6 inches deep (deeper for better pro-

Alstroemeria aurantiaca

Anemone blanda 'Radar'

tection from cold) and about 1 foot apart. Position them among shrubs or perennials, where withering leaves in early summer won't be unsightly, but don't shade the soil above the bulbs. Heat and dryness during the late spring and early summer dormancy are imperative. Because moving a belladonna lily can easily stop its blooming for several years, it is best to divide clumps only when necessary or to move them during or just after blooming, keeping intact around the bulbs as much soil as possible. Use loose, deep mulch where necessary to protect foliage from frost. Propagate by division and offsets. Bulbs in containers should be planted with their tops exposed and allowed to go dry after foliage dies, then watered after midsummer until blooming. Let the plants become potbound.

The plants are poisonous if eaten.

A number of named varieties are sold. Desirable for their evergreen foliage and fine flowers are hybrids between *A. belladonna* and *Crinum* (× *Amarcrinum* or *Crinodonna*, also spelled *Crindonna*), but they are sometimes difficult to obtain.

Amaryllis belladonna

Anemone coronaria

Anemone

Windflower

Buttercup family.
Rhizome or tuber; deciduous.
Bloom time is usually spring, often quite early.

Location: For *A. nemorosa,* woodland; for others, meadow, rock garden, woodland, border, container, alpine house, bulb frame, greenhouse.

Soil: For *A. nemorosa,* well drained, acid to neutral; for others, well drained, neutral to alkaline.

Care: *A. nemorosa* requires year-round moisture; others require moisture during periods of active growth and dryness during dormancy. In areas with summer rainfall, dig and store until fall.

Exposure: For *A. nemorosa,* light shade; for most others, light shade or full sun.

The open-faced, fresh, poppylike beauty and lovely colors of anemones have established them as garden and florist staples. Discussed here are some of the finest rhizomatous species and hybrids; fibrous-rooted species, such as *A.* × *hybrida* (Japanese anemone), have been omitted. As indicated above, *A. nemorosa* requires a different regimen.

Native to the deciduous woodlands of Europe, Britain, and Asia, *A. nemorosa* (European wood anemone) needs the filtered shade, rich organic soil and moisture that its natural habitat provides. In mid- or late spring, 6- to 9-inch stems bear 1-inch, white, silvery lavender, lavender blue, blue, or pink blossoms. It is hardy to –30° F. Where well adapted, it naturalizes freely. Plant rhizomes 3 inches deep, 6 inches apart, in clumps and drifts around trees or shrubbery. Availability from American sources is limited. The plant is poisonous to eat.

The other anemones listed here are species (or hybrids derived from species) whose natural habitats are more southerly and summer dry. They establish best in garden or container situations that approximate those habitats, but they can be grown successfully for a season in the garden or in containers and then discarded, if you prefer. Plant 3 to 4 inches deep and 4 to 6 inches apart. You can grow all of them north of adapted zones if you are willing to dig

Anomatheca laxa

and store them in peat moss or sand, but starting over with fresh rhizomes assures more predictable and satisfactory results. North of their adapted zones, plant in the spring; elsewhere, plant in the fall or spring. These anemones can be propagated by sowing seeds as soon as they are ripened, or by dividing older rhizomes or tubers after the foliage has died back. The flowers close at night.

A. apennina, hardy to 0° F, is from the high, rocky mountain meadows of southern Europe. It is well suited to borders, rock gardens, or lightly shaded woodlands where it can naturalize. On 2- to 9-inch stems, it bears 1-inch starlike blue, rose, or white, single or double flowers in early spring. It prefers some shade.

A. blanda, very similar to *A. apennina,* is from southeastern Europe and Asia Minor; it bears sky-blue, dark blue, white, pink, rose, or blue and white flowers in spring. Several named varieties are widely sold. It should be planted in the fall.

A. coronaria has flowers 2 inches wide or wider on 5- to 10-inch stems. It is the most common garden and florist anemone and is very widely available. Its showy flowers are white, red, blue, or purple, most with contrasting centers. They last 4 to 7 days when cut. You may want to stagger plantings for a longer bloom period. Hybrids of *A. coronaria* are generally showier and larger flowered, to 4 inches wide. *A. coronaria* and its hybrids must be dried off in areas of summer rainfall. All are hardy to 0° F.

A. × *fulgens,* a naturally occurring hybrid from southern Europe, bears black-centered 2-inch scarlet flowers on 6- to 12-inch stems. The St. Bavo strain has 2-inch starlike flowers, ranging from white through pink, salmon, brick red, dark red and violet-blue. *A.* × *fulgens* and its hybrids are hardy to –10° F and bloom in spring.

Arisaema triphyllum

Anomatheca

Iris family.
Corm; deciduous.
Blooms late spring or summer.

Cultural requirements and ornamental uses are identical to those of the closely related *Lapeirousia* (see page 75).

The two species of this African genus most likely to be available occasionally from specialists are spring and summer growing.

A. laxa (*A. cruenta, Lapierousia laxa*) grows 8 to 12 inches tall or sometimes taller and has small scarlet flowers with dark red blotches. A white form is also sold. It does best with some shade.

A. grandiflora (*Laperierousia grandiflora*) is similar to *A. laxa* but bears larger (2-inch) bright red flowers, usually in late spring. Like *L. laxa*, it prefers shade.

Anthericum liliago

St. Bernard's lily

Lily family.
Tuberous roots; deciduous.
Blooms in spring and summer.

Location: Border, meadow, rock garden.

Soil: Well drained, organic, sandy, acid to neutral.

Care: Water regularly and give occasional light feedings with complete fertilizer during growth period.

Exposure: Sun or very light shade.

This lily relative comes from alpine meadows. It bears 1½- to 3-foot plumy spires of starry 1-inch fragrant white flowers with delicately green-tipped petals and prominent yellow anthers. Anthericum is easy to grow where winter low temperatures reach from 0° to 20° F. Roots and seeds are sold by specialists.

Anthericum liliago

Arisaema

Arum family.
Tuber; deciduous.
Blooms in spring or early summer.

Location: Woodland, mixed border, container.

Soil: Well drained, organic, slightly acid.

Care: Water generously; little or no feeding in rich woodland soil.

Exposure: Light to medium shade.

North American jack-in-the-pulpit (*A. triphyllum*) and green dragon, and *A. ringens* from Japan, Korea, and China are fascinating plants well adapted to woodland conditions where winter temperatures do not drop below –20° F. All have glossy, attractive three-lobed leaves that last through the summer. The curious green and purplish brown striped flower (actually a sheath enclosing a greenish column that bears the sexual parts) on close inspection reveals the kinship of arisaema with the calla lily. All produce colorful reddish berries in summer and fall. The native species are available from wildflower specialists. *A. ringens* is more difficult to locate. You may find other species offered by specialists.

Plant the tubers about 4 inches deep and 10 to 24 inches apart in the fall. Propagate from offsets in the fall or start seeds indoors and plant out in the spring or fall.

A. dracontium (green dragon or dragon root), a woodland native of a large area from Maine to Florida and Mexico, grows 1 to 3 feet tall.

A. ringens, from the seaside woodlands in northeastern Asia, grows to 18 inches or taller.

A. triphyllum, from the woodlands of eastern North America, grows 1 to 3 feet tall.

Anthericum
liliago

Arisaema
triphyllum

Arum
italicum

Arum italicum

Arum italicum

Italian arum

Arum family.
Tuber; deciduous.
Blooms in spring or early summer.

Location: Border, woodland edge, container.

Soil: Well drained, organic, acid to neutral.

Care: Water generously, especially through period of growth and blooming; feed occasionally with a complete fertilizer.

Exposure: Sun or light shade.

The attractions of Italian arum include white-marbled, waxy, arrow-shaped 12-inch leaves that appear in the fall and last into spring; creamy or greenish callalike flowers, up to 8 inches long, sometimes spotted or stained at their bases with purple; and (the showiest feature) tight clusters of brilliant scarlet berries that last through the summer. This 12- to 18-inch-tall native of the Mediterranean area has a subtle beauty that invites close inspection. Foliage and berries are excellent for flower arrangements, but they are poisonous if eaten.

Plant tubers in late summer, 2 or 3 inches deep and 6 inches apart. Propagate by division in late summer or seed in fall. The variety 'Pictum' (or 'Marmoratum') has heavily variegated leaves. The species and this variety are usually available from specialists.

Asphodeline lutea

Asphodelus cerasiferus

Asphodeline lutea

(Asphodelus luteus)
Asphodel, Jacob's Rod, King's Spear

Lily family.
Rhizome; deciduous.
Blooms in summer.

Location: Border, woodland.

Soil: Well drained, sandy.

Care: Water regularly and feed lightly with complete fertilizer through period of blooming.

Exposure: Sun or partial shade.

Planted in generous clumps, this free-flowering native of the Mediterranean area contributes bright color and sweet fragrance to the garden over a long summer season. Its 2- to 4-foot spikes are densely covered over the top foot by bracts and star-like yellow blossoms that open in the afternoon. The bottoms of the spikes are surrounded by narrow leaves. Asphodelus is occasionally sold by some general suppliers as well as specialists. A double form is less available but well worth a search.

Asphodeline lutea

Asphodelus cerasiferus

Plant the rhizomes 3 to 4 inches deep and 18 inches apart, or sow the easy-to-germinate seeds outdoors in the spring. Propagate by division. Clumps bloom best when left undisturbed for several years.

Asphodelus cerasiferus

Asphodel

Lily family.
Rhizome; deciduous.
Blooms in early summer.

Cultural requirements and garden uses of *Asphodelus* are identical with those of closely related *Asphodeline*.

Native to the Mediterranean area, asphodel bears a strong family resemblance to its cousin described above. This species forms many-branched flower spikes 4 to 5 feet tall, topped by 1-inch fragrant white blossoms with brownish petal backs and bright orange anthers. Its gray green leaves are longer and broader than those of its cousin. It is seldom sold in this country.

Babiana

Baboon flower

Iris family.
Corm; deciduous.
Blooms in spring in the garden, in winter or early spring indoors or under glass.

Location: Rock garden, border, container, alpine house, house, greenhouse.

Soil: Most fast-draining garden soils.

Care: Water regularly during period of growth and blooming; dry off after leaves turn brown. In wet-summer areas, dig and store in dry packing material in a warm place until cool weather of autumn. Feed lightly early in the growing period.

Exposure: Sun or very light shade.

Baboon flower—so called because, in its native South Africa, baboons eat its corms—is one of the choicest bulbs for garden or container and, given the proper environment, one of the easiest to grow. Flowers vary in shape from regularly round to two-sectioned, each section comprising three petals of unequal size. The upright 1- to 2-inch blossoms (some are larger, as noted below) are borne in short, dense spikes, rising in some species above fans of short, pleated, swordlike, and rather fuzzy leaves. Other species bear flowers close to the bases of the plants. Predominant flower colors in this large genus are shades of red, blue, mauve, and yellow, as well as cream and white. Many are beautifully marked. Some are fragrant. With winter mulching in protected southern exposures, babiana thrives in dry-summer areas where the winter

Babiana villosa

temperature drops as low as 0° F. It is an attractive, easy-to-grow container plant for any climate. Babiana, particularly its hybrid varieties, is widely sold by specialists.

After the onset of cool autumn weather, plant corms in the garden 5 to 9 inches deep and 2 inches apart. Plant up to 10 or 12 corms per 6-inch pot; position them as deep as is feasible. Divide only when the plants become crowded. Propagate from offsets in fall, or from seed.

In addition to the many named hybrids, here are a few especially attractive and easy-to-grow species.

B. ambigua bears its blossoms on a short spike, usually 2 inches high. The flowers are an intensely beautiful blue or blue mauve with white or pale yellow areas and a prominent purple marking.

B. disticha (*B. plicata*) grows 3 to 8 inches high and has flowers varying from purple to violet, pale blue, or white, with a yellow or white area often marked with two purple dots.

B. nana, whose spikes grow to 4 inches high, has 3-inch cuplike, blue to rose pink flowers with a yellow or white area and a purple or reddish purple arrow-shaped marking.

B. pygmaea is usually about 3 inches tall and has 4-inch cream or sulfur yellow flowers with a narrow purple-maroon blotch at the base.

B. rubrocyanea (*B. stricta* var. *rubrocyanea*) grows 5 to 8 inches tall and has purplish blue flowers with crimson centers.

B. stricta, the best-known babiana, is 8 to 12 inches tall and has purple, bluish mauve, royal blue, and sometimes yellow flowers with purple markings at the base. Many of the babiana hybrids are derived from *B. stricta*.

B. villosa grows to 15 inches tall and has cup-shaped, reddish wine flowers with thick black anthers. It sometimes requires staking.

Picotee begonia 'Fairylike'

Begonia × tuberhybrida

Tuberous begonia

Begonia family.
Tuber; deciduous.
Blooms early summer to fall.

Location: Container, border, greenhouse, house.

Soil: Well drained, organic, acid to neutral.

Care: Water and feed regularly with complete fertilizer during period of active growth and blooming. Gradually dry off when leaves start to yellow, and store tubers cool in dry packing material or in their pots.

Exposure: Light shade.

Hybrid tuberous begonias, whose ancestors are native to the Andes, provide unrivaled brilliance  through the warm months. The flowers are large, showy, variable in form (see the classification of flower form below) and clear and bright in color. The color range excludes only blue, green, and purple; bicolors are common. Each bloom stem bears small, single female flowers and large—to 6 inches wide—single or double male flowers. Some varieties are perfect for hanging planters, others for pots and beds. Tuberous begonias are in their element in humid, cool-summer climates.

In late winter or early spring, plant tubers in a frost-free spot, stem side up, so that their tops are slightly above soil level. Or you can plant seedlings, which are frequently sold in 2-inch pots. For earlier blooms, start begonias indoors and move them outside when the weather permits. Flowers will face in the direction that the leaves point. Use three or four tubers or seedlings per hanging basket; in beds space them 10 to 18 inches apart. Water regularly, but avoid overhead watering because tuberous begonias are highly susceptible to mildew. Guard against slugs and snails. Propagate by seeds, starting them indoors early in the year; by shoot or leaf cuttings in the spring; or by division.

The following list of common forms of tuberous begonias uses terms common in most catalogs to classify the varieties. Some groups may overlap (for example, *Crispa* and *Marginata*).

Camellia-form varieties are upright (and, like most upright types, 12 to 18 inches tall) and bear large double flowers resembling double camellias. There are also ruffled-camellia-form varieties.

Carnation-form varieties are similar to camellia-form ones, except that the dense, crisp petals resemble those of carnations.

Crispa varieties bear large single flowers with frilled and ruffled petal edges.

Cristata (crested) varieties bear large single flowers with a frilly crest near the center of each petal.

Babiana stricta

Belamcanda chinensis

Marginata varieties are like the Picotee group except that the petals are bordered with a sharply contrasting color.

Marmorata varieties are similar to the camellia-form group, but they are rose colored and blotched or spotted with white.

Multiflora tuberous begonias are low, compact plants with 2-inch single or double flowers. They accept a bit more sun than most other types.

Nonstop varieties, usually available as seedlings, bear single, double, and semidouble flowers together and are especially free flowering.

Pendula (hanging basket) varieties have a pendulous habit to 18 inches and bloom heavily. Flowers are single or double, small or large. The Sensation begonias have large double flowers.

Picotee varieties bear large, camellia-form flowers in which the color changes by gradations toward the petal edges.

Rose-form varieties bear flowers with smooth-edged petals and furled centers, like those of double roses.

*Begonia ×
tuberhybrida*

Belamcanda chinensis

(Pardanthus chinensis)
Blackberry lily, Leopard flower

Iris family.
Rhizome; deciduous.
Blooms in summer.

Location: Border, container.

Soil: Rich, sandy loam.

Care: Water during active growth; no fertilizing is needed.

Exposure: Full sun or light shade.

This undemand-
ing native of China and Japan is valued for its imposing flat fans of foliage, 2-inch crimson-speckled orange flowers borne on 2- to 3-foot branching stems over a long season during summer, and clusters of shiny black berries revealed when the pods split in the fall. The berries are attractive in dried arrangements. Where winters don't get colder than –10° F, belamcanda can be used to add texture and color to perennial and mixed borders. It can be grown in the ground or in containers in any climate, then either dug or left in the containers and stored in a frost-free location during the winter.

Plant in the garden in spring or early fall, 1 inch deep and 6 inches apart. Blooming is more profuse in full sun, though blackberry lily accepts light shade. Except in mild-winter areas, give it winter mulch. Propagate by division, or by sowing seeds outdoors in the spring or summer, up to 2 months before the first frost.

B. chinensis is widely sold. Occasionally you may find that *B. flabellata* is offered by a specialist. It is quite similar to *B. chinensis,* except that flowers are pure yellow and it prefers some shade and frequent watering. Recently developed × *Pardancanda norrisii,* a hybrid between *Belamcanda* and *Pardanthopsis,* has uses and cultural needs similar to those of *B. chinensis.* Flowers are solid or speckled, blotched, and sometimes bicolored, in a rainbow of colors. It is becoming available from some general nurseries.

*Belamcanda
chinensis*

Bessera elegans

Bessera elegans

Coral drops

Amaryllis family.
True bulb; deciduous.
Blooms midsummer to autumn outdoors, spring or early summer indoors.

Location: Border, container, meadow, alpine house, greenhouse, house.

Soil: Well drained, sandy, organic, acid to neutral.

Care: Water generously during active growth, spring and summer; dry off after flowering. Feed lightly with a complete fertilizer during growth period.

Exposure: Sun.

It's a pity that
this showy, elegant flower from Mexico is so seldom offered commercially. Wiry 2- to 3-foot stems bear loose clusters of nodding, 1¾-inch, scarlet, coral, or purple flowers with white stripes inside. The leaves are grasslike and narrow, to nearly 3 feet long. In borders and garden meadows where the temperature doesn't drop below 10° F, bessera can be a perennial feature. Elsewhere it must be dried off, dug, and stored warm in dry packing medium in the fall, then replanted in early spring. It is easy to grow as a container plant, which can be dried off in the pot in a warm spot during the winter.

In the fall plant corms 4 inches deep and 7 to 8 inches apart in the garden where plants will receive summer sun and wind won't break the long stems. If you grow bessera in containers indoors or outdoors, plant three or four bulbs per 8-inch pot. Propagate in the fall from offsets.

*Bessera
elegans*

Triteleia laxa

Brodiaea, Dichelostemma, and Triteleia

Amaryllis family.
Corm; deciduous.
Blooms spring or early summer.

Location: Rock garden, border, meadow, woodland, container, alpine house.

Soil: Very well drained and sandy, particularly where any summer rain is likely.

Care: Water regularly during growth period, from late fall to early spring; then dry off until mid- or late fall.

Exposure: Sun.

One of North America's loveliest contributions to horticulture is the brodiaea (many of which have recently been divided into the genera *Dichelostemma* or *Triteleia*). Flowers are borne in tight or loose clusters atop leafless stems, and colors in the blue, lavender, and purple range predominate, though there are interesting exceptions. With winter mulching and warm exposures, most brodiaeas can be grown outdoors where winter temperatures dip as low as –20° F. They are attractive in large, massed, informal plantings. Rainless summers are best for them, but with good drainage they will generally survive some rain. In wet-summer areas they can be dug and stored in a packing material. Brodiaeas are excellent cut flowers. Some species and the hybrids are rather widely sold; others are occasionally offered by specialists.

Plant corms 3 to 5 inches deep and 3 inches apart in the fall, or plant four or five corms 2 inches deep in a 6-inch pot. Propagate from offsets or seeds in the fall.

The following are the best brodiaea species for cultivation, listed in the approximate order of blooming. They are listed under their current genus names, which are abbreviated, but most are sold as *Brodiaea*.

D. pulchellum (combining the former *B. pulchella* and *B. capitata*), blue-dicks, in early spring produces tight clusters of blue or blue violet flowers on 1½- to 2½-foot stems.

B. lutea (*T. ixioides*, *B. ixioides*), golden brodiaea or pretty face, blooms golden yellow. Stems are up to 15 feet tall.

T. laxa (*B. laxa*), Ithuriel's spear, the most widely sold brodiaea, has large violet-purple, blue, or white flowers in graceful, loose umbels atop stems to 30 inches tall. Bloom time varies from early to late spring. The variety 'Queen Fabiola', usually about 1 foot tall, has deep blue flowers with light blue midribs. It is widely available.

In late spring to early summer these species begin to bloom:

T. hyacinthina (*B. hyacinthina*) bears white flowers, sometimes with a bluish cast, in relatively loose umbels atop stems from 1 to 2 feet high. Some selections of this species accept water in the garden better than most other brodiaeas do.

B. elegans bears purple-violet blooms in open umbels on stems to 18 inches high. The petals are extraordinarily substantial.

B. coronaria, harvest brodiaea, bears a wide umbel of rose-violet flowers atop a 1-foot stem.

D. ida-maia (*B. ida-maia*), firecracker flower, stands out from other brodiaeas in form and coloration. Rather pendulous bright red tubes with flaring green tips and a white center bloom atop 1- to 3-foot stems.

Triteleia uniflora is now called *Ipheion uniflorum*. See page 72.

Brodiaea hyacinthina

Bulbinella floribunda

Lily family.
Tuberous roots; deciduous.
Blooms late winter to early spring.

Location: Border.

Soil: Well drained, sandy, acid to neutral.

Bulbinella floribunda

Care: Water generously through period of growth and blooming, in late fall, winter, and spring; water occasionally in summer as long as soil is very well drained. No feeding is necessary.

Exposure: Sun or light shade.

Delightful in gardens that stay warmer than 10° F (it is an undemanding, beautiful winter bloomer) and in vases (its blossoms last up to two weeks), bulbinella deserves greater prominence in horticulture. Unfortunately, this South African bulb is seldom sold in the United States. Its pokerlike 2- to 3-foot spikes of densely clustered, daffodil yellow (or sometimes orange, cream, or white) flowers are held above narrow, arching 2-foot leaves.

Plant bulbinella seeds in the fall (they germinate in about 10 days), or propagate in the fall from offsets. Sow seeds in pots of moist medium in light shade, and keep the medium moist until the dormant season, when it must still not be allowed to dry completely. Seedlings can be planted out the following fall. Plant tuberous roots just beneath soil level.

Bulbinella floribunda

Bulbocodium vernum

Bulbocodium vernum

Spring meadow saffron

Lily family.
Corm; deciduous.
Blooms late winter or early spring.

Location: Rock garden, meadow, container.

Soil: Well drained, sandy, acid to neutral.

Care: Water regularly after blooming, until leaves start to wither; too much winter water can be harmful. No fertilizing is necessary in most garden soils.

Exposure: Sun.

Among the earliest flowers of the season, along with winter aconite and the early crocuses, bulbocodium bursts into bloom before its leaves emerge. Light reddish purple, 4-inch-tall flowers with white centers resemble those of colchicum, which is a close relative, and crocus; sometimes two or three flowers emerge from one corm. When flowers are fully developed, 6-inch leaves emerge. Native to the Alps and other mountains of southern Europe and Asia Minor, bulbocodium is extremely hardy.

In the fall plant corms 4 to 5 inches deep and 3 to 4 inches apart in clumps or drifts. Plant five or six bulbs in a 6-inch pot or bulb pan. Dig and divide every two or three years. Propagate in the fall from offsets. Bulbocodium is available from some specialists in the fall.

Bulbocodium vernum

Caladium × hortulanum

Caladium × hortulanum

Fancy-leaved caladium

Arum family.
Tuber; deciduous.
Blooms in summer; leaves—not flowers—are decorative.

Location: Border, container, house, greenhouse.

Soil: Well drained, organic, acid to neutral.

Care: Give ample water and feed with complete fertilizer during growing period. Gradually dry off in early fall; where temperature drops below 20° F, dig tubers when foliage has died; air for a few days, then store at 70° F or leave in dry pots.

Exposure: Light to deep shade.

Large, extravagantly colored and patterned, sometimes nearly translucent leaves, not flowers, are the great attraction of caladium hybrids, whose parents grow in South American jungles. In any location where summer night temperatures seldom drop below 60° F, they add bold strokes of color to shady garden areas. In any climate zone, they are choice seasonal houseplants; by planting tubers in several pots at two- or three-month intervals, you can enjoy the beauty of caladiums the year around indoors. These 1- to 3-foot-tall plants bear bicolored or tricolored leaves. One color fades into another; or veins, borders, or spatterings of color contrast with adjacent colors; or both. White and green; red and green; red, rose, and green; pink and green; and red and metallic green are among the array of combinations. Dozens of named varieties are widely available.

Either wait until soil and night temperatures are warm (around 60° F) before planting, or start tubers early indoors, using soil-heating cables to keep the growing medium at 70° to 85° F. In the ground or pots, place the tubers knobby side up beneath 2 inches of soil. Plant one large tuber or two or three small tubers per 8-inch pot. In garden beds, space 8 to 12 inches apart. As long as good drainage can be maintained, an easy growing technique is to start the tubers in pots, plunge the pots into garden beds, then lift the pots for dry storage at 70° F during dormancy. Or you can store bare tubers from beds or planters in dry packing material. Propagate by division during dormancy. Snails and slugs are a real threat.

Caladium × hortulanum

Calochortus venustus

Calochortus

Lily family.
True bulb; deciduous.
Blooms late spring and early summer.

Location: Rock garden, container, alpine house, dry-summer meadow.

Soil: Well drained, sandy, acid to neutral, not too rich.

Care: After cool weather begins in late fall, water regularly until flowering, then completely dry off until fall; no fertilizing is necessary in most garden soils.

Exposure: Sun or light shade, depending on species.

Mariposa lilies, fairy lanterns, and star tulips are among the common names of these natives of the western United States. Most need protection from alternate freezing and thawing (winter mulching helps). Plant the bulbs in late fall, 3 to 5 inches deep in the garden, or 2 to 4 inches deep in pots, five or six bulbs per 6-inch pot. Unless you want to collect the seeds, pinch the ovary off after each flower fades in order to conserve vigor for blooming the next season. Lift and store in dry packing material any bulbs that would be wet by summer or early fall rains. Container-grown calochortuses can be dried off and stored in their containers. Propagate from offsets or seeds in the fall; dry off seedlings during the dormant period.

Mariposa lilies, also called Mariposa tulips and butterfly tulips, the showiest group of calochortuses, grow up to 2½ feet or more. The three broad, fan-shaped petals of most species curve gracefully backward at their edges and are splendidly marked and feathered. The following are several Mariposa lilies that you can probably locate with some persistence.

C. catalinae has white flowers tinged with lilac or pale purple, with a purple blotch at each petal base.

C. luteus (yellow Mariposa), has rich yellow flowers, speckled and lined with red brown toward the center of the flower, often with a dark blotch on each petal.

C. superbus bears white to yellowish or lavender flowers, often streaked with purple toward the center, with a reddish brown or red blotch surrounded by yellow.

C. venustus (white Mariposa), perhaps the most famous of the calochortuses, is quite variable in coloration with white, yellow, purple, or red petals, usually marked with a dark red blotch toward the center; some have red blotches on the tips.

C. vestae bears white to purplish flowers with russet streaks toward the center and reddish brown blotches surrounded by yellow.

Fairy lanterns, or globe tulips, grow 1 to 2½ feet tall and bear nodding, globular, 1-inch flowers with fringed petals that are very hairy inside toward their bases. This group of calochortuses prefers light shade. The following are sold occasionally.

C. albus bears white flowers, sometimes delicately rose tinted.

C. amabilis has rich yellow flowers that in silhouette are nearly triangular.

Star tulips or pussy-ears, up to 12 inches tall, have upright flowers, often with long hairs on their petals. They prefer partial shade. The latter of the following species is sold fairly often by specialists, the former less often.

C. tolmiei has white or cream flowers, sometimes tinted rose, lavender, or purple.

C. uniflorus has white or lilac flowers with a purple spot near the base of each petal. Like *C. amoenus*, it tolerates more water than most calochortuses.

The following two species from Canada and the Northwest are suitable for garden cultivation in a cold-winter climate, but you may have trouble locating a source.

C. eurycarpus grows to 20 inches tall and bears upright 3-inch flowers that are gleaming white, rarely pale lavender, with a prominent purple spot in the center of each petal.

C. macrocarpus (green-banded Mariposa) grows to 20 inches and bears 4-inch purple flowers with a green stripe on each petal and sometimes a purple band around the hairy center of each flower.

Camassia esculente

Calochortus amabilis

Camassia quamash

Camassia

Camass, Camas
Lily family.
True bulb; deciduous.
Blooms in late spring.

Location: Meadow, woodland, border.

Soil: Most soils, including heavy, wet types.

Care: Water generously during active growth and blooming. No fertilizer is necessary.

Exposure: Sun or light shade.

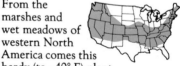

From the marshes and wet meadows of western North America comes this hardy (to −40° F) plant that produces grassy leaves and airy spikes of 1- to 1½-inch starlike blossoms. Planted in masses, camass makes a delightful display during spring. Camass is an unassuming, easy plant that tolerates neglect and a wide range of cultural conditions. You can buy it from specialists and some general suppliers.

Plant bulbs in early fall, 4 to 5 inches deep and 3 to 4 inches apart. Propagate from offsets or from seeds sown in the spring.

C. leichtlinii, native from British Columbia to northern California, bears deep blue-violet to bright blue flowers on stems to 3 or 4 feet tall. Semidouble white and single dark blue forms are sold.

C. quamash (*C. esculenta*), called quamash, from the same area as *C. leichtlinii*, bears deep blue-violet 2-inch flowers on 1½- to 2-foot stems.

Canna hortensis

Canna

Canna, Indian-shot
Canna family.
Rhizome; deciduous.
Blooms late spring to fall.

Location: Border, container.

Soil: Any rich, organic, well-drained soil (but will survive in poor soil).

Care: Feed and water regularly throughout the growing season.

Exposure: Sun.

Large and smooth, green, bronze, or variegated leaves of canna create a luxurious tropical effect in the garden, suggesting their origins in the jungles of the New World. Massed in beds, clumped in the border, or filling tubs or pots on the terrace or beside a pool, they contribute not just handsome greenery but constant, bold color during the warm months. White, scarlet, apricot, coral, pink, yellow, and variegated varieties are sold individually and as mixes. Heights vary from around 18 inches (for example the Seven Dwarfs strain) to 24 to 36 inches (Pfitzer's Dwarfs) to 3 or 4 feet or taller (Crozy or French cannas). Where the winters don't get below 20° F, canna generally naturalizes and can be left in the ground. Where winters are colder than this, mulch the rhizomes heavily, or, where winter temperatures drop below 10° F, lift and store them during the cold.

Plant rhizomes in the spring, when the soil has warmed, 3 to 4 inches deep and, depending on the variety, from 1½ to 3 feet apart. Divide every three or four years. Propagate in the spring by division, or nick each seed with a nail file, soak it 24 to 48 hours in warm water, then sow in the ground or a pot at 70° to 75° F. In the fall, once the tops have dried, store the rhizomes dry at 50° to 60° F. Watch for snails and slugs, which can be particularly damaging.

Cardiocrinum giganteum

Cardiocrinum giganteum

Lily family.
True bulb; deciduous.
Blooms in summer.

Location: Border, woodland.

Soil: Cool, well drained, organic, acid to neutral.

Care: Water regularly (watering may be reduced a bit during dormancy) and feed regularly with a complete fertilizer during active growth.

Exposure: Partial shade.

One of the largest and most imposingly handsome of the bulbs, cardiocrinum grows 6 to 12 feet, its sparsely leaved stem rising from a striking rosette of 10-inch-wide, heart-shaped leaves and bearing up to 25, 6-inch-long, fragrant, white, nodding trumpets striped inside with reddish purple. For a shaded border or woodland area in a spacious garden, nothing could be more effective than this Himalayan native. The huge bulbs die after blooming but leave behind a cluster of offsets. A well-established planting blooms every year. Cardiocrinum is hardy to –10 °F. Unfortunately, it is still very difficult to locate in the United States.

Plant the huge bulbs beneath only 1 inch of soil. Mulch in winter in cold areas. Propagate by offsets in the fall or by seeds planted indoors in early fall for germination in spring.

Canna indica

Cardiocrinum giganteum

Chasmanthe aethiopica

Chasmanthe aethiopica

Chasmanthe

Iris family.
Corm; deciduous.
Blooms in spring or summer.

Location: Border, container, meadow.

Soil: Any well-drained garden soil.

Care: Chasmanthe survives complete neglect where adapted but looks best with regular watering and light feeding with complete fertilizer during growth period. Dry off after blooming stops; it will tolerate late-summer and autumn rain if soil drains quickly.

Exposure: Sun or light shade.

Easily confused with similar-looking *Crocosmia × crocosmiifolia* and some *Tritonia* species, this large-scale South African has fans of bold, swordlike foliage and flower spikes 2 to 5 feet tall. Narrow, tubular flowers, usually red and orange, grow along the upper portions of the spikes. This old-fashioned garden favorite is now seldom available commercially.

Plant corms in the spring or fall, 4 inches deep and 8 to 12 inches apart. Where it isn't hardy, dry off, dig, and store the corms in dry packing material over the winter. For container culture, plant the corms 2 inches deep. Propagate by division or offsets in spring or fall, or by seeds sown indoors in early spring. Dry off the seedlings during dormancy, and plant out the following spring.

Two very similar species are sometimes available. *C. aethiopica* has spikes of flowers all facing in the same direction. It is hardy to 0° F. *C. floribunda*, which has broader leaves and flowers facing in two directions on each spike, is hardy to 20° F.

Clivia miniata

Chionodoxa 'Spring Beauty'

Chlidanthus fragrans

Chionodoxa

Glory-of-the-snow

Lily family.
True bulb; deciduous.
Blooms late winter or early spring.

Location: Meadow, rock garden, alpine house, seasonally indoors.

Soil: Acid to neutral, sandy loam or scree is ideal, but most well-drained garden soils are adequate.

Care: Water during period of growth. Little or no fertilizer.

Exposure: Sun; light shade in hot climates.

An early bloom season and easy adaptability to a wide range of growing conditions make this native of the high mountain meadows of Asia Minor desirable where winters get as cold as –20° F. Easily naturalized in clumps and drifts, it suits most informal garden styles. It can be forced for midwinter blooming.

Plant the bulbs 4 to 5 inches deep in early fall, spacing them about 3 inches apart, or using 12 to 15 per 8-inch bulb pan. Propagate by offsets in early fall or by seeds.

Two recommended species are widely available. The more common, *C. luciliae*, varies in height from 3 to 6 inches and includes varieties (some sold as *C. gigantea*) with white or white-eyed blue or pink flowers, to 1¾ inches wide, 6 to 10 per stem. Similar in appearance is *C. sardensis*, which has sky-blue flowers on 4- to 6-inch stems.

Chlidanthus fragrans

Perfumed fairy lily

Amaryllis family.
True bulb; deciduous.
Blooms in summer.

Location: Rock garden, container.

Soil: Most well drained, sandy garden soils.

Care: Water generously and feed lightly with a complete fertilizer during period of growth and blooming, then dry off until spring.

Exposure: Sun.

As many as four intensely fragrant, funnel-shaped, pale yellow flowers, 3 to 4 inches long on a foot-tall stem make this native of the Andes a delightful choice for year-round garden culture where winters don't get colder than 10° F, and for seasonal or container planting elsewhere. It is an excellent cut flower. Chlidanthus is occasionally offered by specialists.

As early as possible in the spring, plant bulbs 3 inches deep and 16 to 20 inches apart in the garden, or with the tips of the bulbs barely exposed in containers, 1 bulb per 6-inch pot. Dry off as foliage starts to wither; where chlidanthus isn't hardy, dig or remove bulbs from pots and store in a cool spot in dry packing material. Propagate from offsets, or sow seeds in the spring for bloom in four or five years.

Chionodoxa luciliae

Chlidanthus fragrans

Clivia miniata

Clivia miniata

Kaffir lily

Amaryllis family.
Bulbous root; evergreen.
Blooms late winter or spring.

Location: House, greenhouse, border.

Soil: Well drained, organic, acid to neutral.

Care: Water and feed with a complete fertilizer regularly during active growth and flowering; afterward, stop feeding, and water minimally.

Exposure: Partial to deep shade.

One of the brightest flowers for indoors and shady corners of the garden is kaffir lily, whose deep green, strap leaves are assets the year around. This South African bears an umbel of 12 to 20 flowers atop each 12- to 18-inch bloom stalk. Flowers are typically orange with yellowish centers, but scarlet, deep red, salmon, yellow, and gold and white forms are sometimes sold. The bright red berries are attractive.

You can plant kaffir lily in any season, though the period just after flowering is best. Set the bulbous roots just beneath the soil. You will find that a plant blooms better as it becomes root-bound, so leave it in its place in the garden or container as long as possible, dividing it only when it becomes too crowded. Protect it from cold night temperatures and from direct sun (though deep shade makes for light blooming). Clivia is easily propagated by division, and by fresh seeds sown in a moist medium kept at 80° to 85° F. Plants are sold by many general suppliers; seeds are sometimes sold in protective capsules.

Colchicum autumnale 'Water Lily'

Colocasia esculentum

Colchicum

Autumn crocus

Lily family.
Corm; deciduous.
Blooms in fall.

Location: Meadow, woodland, rock garden, container seasonally indoors.

Soil: Sandy, organic, acid to neutral is best, but any well-drained garden soil will do.

Care: Water during period of active growth; no fertilizing is necessary in garden soil.

Exposure: Partial shade or full sun.

This lily family lookalike of crocus, a member of the iris family, serves much the same function in the autumn that true crocus serves in early spring: providing a burst of brilliance in a drab season. Used informally in broad drifts or random-sized clumps, this 4- to 8-inch-tall native of the Mediterranean area and parts of Asia makes dazzling patches of amethyst, mauve, pink, rose, violet, purple, or white. Flowers are 2 to 8 inches wide and flowering lasts for a couple of weeks. Several months later, in the winter or spring, the lush, straplike leaves appear, growing to about 1 foot high, then dying after a few weeks—so be sure to plant colchicum where the foliage won't be unsightly in its annual decline.

Plant corms during dormancy, in late summer or early fall, under 3 to 4 inches of soil, 6 to 9 inches apart. You can bring container-grown plants indoors during flowering. You can even set bare corms in saucers of pebbles indoors and enjoy the splendid flowers that rise quickly from them, but it is usually impossible to transfer these corms to the garden. Colchicum can be propagated by division or removal of cormlets during the dormant period in summer. Frost-free areas don't have enough winter cold for them to naturalize. Divide only when it becomes crowded. Colchicum corms are poisonous if eaten.

The following are some of the most beautiful members of this genus. Most are moderately available in late summer or early fall.

C. agrippinum bears medium-sized, star-shaped, violet-amethyst flowers checkered with white. It naturalizes rapidly where winters do not fall below –10° F. A similar, seldom-available species is C. *variegatum*.

C. autumnale bears a profusion of medium to large flowers. Mauve and white single forms as well as violet-amethyst and white double forms are sold. It is hardy to –20° F.

C. byzantinum bears many rather globular, bright mauve flowers on long white tubes. A white, purple-tinged form is also available. C. *byzantinum* is perhaps the best colchicum for blooming on saucers of pebbles. It is hardy to 0° F.

C. speciosum is the largest and most popular of autumn crocuses. It is available in several named varieties, including 'Album' (pure white, and hard to find), 'Lilac Wonder' (amethyst-violet with white lines in the center), 'The Giant' (violet with a white base), and 'Water lily' (double, amethyst-pink). C. *speciosum* is hardy to –20° F.

Colchicum macrophyllum

Colocasia esculenta

Colocasia esculenta

Elephant's Ear, Taro

Arum family.
Tuber; evergreen in frost-free areas, deciduous elsewhere.
Blooms inconspicuously in summer; leaves, not flowers, are decorative.

Location: Border, container, greenhouse.

Soil: Rich, organic, acid to neutral. Tolerates wetness, even standing water.

Care: Water generously and feed regularly with complete fertilizer.

Exposure: Sun or light shade.

As a specimen in a tub or a large-scale component of a tropical planting perhaps including tree fern, flowering ginger, gloriosa lily, and cup of gold, colocasia is one of the most imposing of garden plants. No matter that its blossoms are insignificant; velvety green 2-foot leaves on a 3- to 7-foot plant are attraction enough. Tubers of this tropical Asian native are a staple in the diet of millions of people from India to the South Pacific. It is a fast-growing, dramatic addition to ornamental gardens as well, even in climates where it must be dug and stored over winter.

Plant tubers 2 to 3 inches deep and up to 6 feet apart. For a longer season in the garden in most of the country, start the tubers indoors in spring, four to six weeks before night temperatures reach 60° F. Start the tubers like those of its colorful cousin caladium, and store them similarly (see page 46). Propagate by division in the spring. Colocasia is widely sold by general suppliers.

Convallaria majalis

Corydalis bulbosa

Corydalis bulbosa

(*C. solida*)
Fumewort

Fumitory family.
Tuber; deciduous.
Blooms in spring.

Location: Woodland, border, rock garden.

Soil: Well drained, organic, acid to neutral.

Care: Water regularly during growth and blooming, the same or less the rest of the year. No fertilizing is necessary.

Exposure: Sun or light shade.

One of the subtler of bulbs, fumewort adds freshness and soft color to early-season plantings. This native of European and Asian woodlands is closely related to bleeding-heart and Dutchman's-breeches. It produces 3- to 9-inch stems of small tubular flowers like snapdragons, varying from white or creamy gray to purple, rose, or lilac, among lush blue-green leaves similar to those of maidenhair fern. Where well adapted, it often naturalizes. It is widely sold by specialists.

Plant tubers 3 inches deep and 4 or 5 inches apart in the fall. Propagate by division.

Convallaria majalis

Lily-of-the-valley

Lily family.
Rhizome; deciduous.
Blooms late spring.

Location: Woodland, border, container, seasonally indoors for forcing, bulb frame for outdoor forcing.

Soil: Most are acceptable, but rich, organic, acid to neutral is best.

Care: Water regularly the year around; feed with complete fertilizer in fall after the first frost.

Exposure: Shade or partial shade; accepts sun in mild-summer areas.

A favorite for vases, bridal bouquets, indoor pots in winter or early spring, and the garden—in woodland plantings, borders, or as a ground cover—lily-of-the-valley is universally valued for its delicate beauty and incomparable fragrance. This native of deciduous woodlands around the North Temperate Zone naturalizes where it gets some winter freezing, and is hardy to –40° F. Where it is well adapted, it forms dense seasonal mats of bold, oval, clear-green leaves. Nodding bell-shaped flowers appear for only a few weeks, but foliage persists from spring to fall. Most of these widely available, 6- to 8-inch-tall plants bear several pure white single flowers, but one cultivar bears mauve ones, another bears double white flowers, and a third has variegated leaves.

Plant the plumpest pips (single rhizomes with growth buds) or clumps from early to midfall. Set the pips 4 to 6 inches apart and 1 to 3 inches deep, and water well. Mulch every fall. Propagate by dividing into smaller clumps or single pips in the fall.

To force indoors, bring in pips after at least two months of frosty weather, or store soilless pips in a plastic bag in the refrigerator for eight weeks. Then pot, with pips just beneath the surface of the soil. To force early blooms in the garden for cutting, place a portable frame over a clump or patch about two months before normal bloom time.

Convallaria majalis

Corydalis bulbosa

Crinum bulbispermum

Crinum

Crinum lily, Spider lily

Amaryllis family.
True bulb; deciduous.
Blooms spring, summer, or fall.

Location: Border, container, greenhouse, house.

Soil: Well drained, deep, organic, acid to neutral.

Care: Water and feed generously with complete fertilizer during growth and flowering; stop feeding and reduce watering when leaves begin to yellow; dry off for winter if necessary, dig, and store in packing material in a moderately warm place.

Exposure: Sun or light shade.

Crinum species come from various warm areas of the world, from the southeastern United States to the Caribbean, South America, South Africa, and tropical Asia. This imposing bulb somewhat resembles its cousin, *Amaryllis belladonna*. Lilylike white, pink, reddish, or bicolored flowers are borne in loose clusters atop thick stalks. Most have a spicy fragrance. Long, arching leaves form large clumps. Crinum is a traditional border and tub plant in the southeastern United States, and some species are hardy enough for year-round garden cultivation where winters get as cold as –20° F. You can buy bulbs from specialists.

Bulbs are sold the year around, but the best time to buy and plant is during the spring or fall dormancy. Set the large bulbs 5 or 6 inches deep and a foot apart. Where hardy, leave

bulbs undisturbed for years. Mulch for winter protection if necessary. For container culture, place each bulb in soil with the neck exposed, in a pot with a diameter only 2 inches greater than that of the bulb. Allow to become thoroughly root-bound before repotting. Propagate in fall from offsets.

The two following crinums are hardy, with protection, to –20° F.

C. bulbispermum (*C. capense, C. longifolium*), from South Africa, in the summer bears 6 to 12 flowers that are pink or white inside and red outside. Plants are 2 to 4 feet tall. *C. × powellii*, a hybrid of *C. bulbispermum*, bears umbels of 6 to 10 rose-pink flowers in the summer. Other color forms are sometimes sold.

The following two crinums are hardy to –10° F, with protection.

C. americanum, from our Southeast, bears two to six white, very fragrant flowers per 2-foot stem, in the winter or spring, before the leaves have emerged.

C. asiaticum, called poison bulb, from tropical Asia, forms large clumps and bears 20 to 50 white flowers per 3-foot stem in the summer. Some forms have a pinkish cast. They are heavily scented in the evening.

The following tender species is suited only to indoor culture or to gardens where winter temperatures do not drop below 10° F.

C. amabile bears 20 to 30 fragrant flowers, bright red outside and pink inside, on 2- to 4-foot stems in the fall. It is native to Sumatra.

You may also find × *Amarcrinum* (× *Crindonna*) offered for sale. See *Amaryllis belladonna*, page 39.

Crinum distichum

Crocosmia × crocosmiiflora

(*Tritonia × crocosmiiflora*)
Montebretia

Iris family.
Corm; deciduous.
Blooms summer and early fall.

Location: Border, meadow.

Soil: Any well-drained garden soil.

Care: Water and feed regularly during period of growth and blooming, though crocosmia is drought tolerant.

Exposure: Sun or light shade.

An old-fashioned garden favorite of central and southern African parentage, this hybrid—together with a multitude of hybrids developed from it and other closely related bulbs—is occasionally sold by general suppliers. Unfortunately, though, its popularity has waned. A few named hybrid varieties are sold, and the choice Earlham hybrids are sometimes available. Where winter temperatures don't fall below 0° F, montebretia is one of the most carefree bulbs, even naturalizing in mildwinter areas and spreading beyond the garden. Leaves are narrow and swordlike, forming dense, spreading clumps. Thin, branching, 3- to 4-foot stems bear 1½- to 3-inch, scarlet to orange flowers. Flowers of some hybrids are even larger, to 4 inches wide, and include salmon, yellow, crimson, maroon, and bicolors. Montebretia is an excellent cut flower lasting more than a week.

Plant corms 3 to 5 inches deep and 6 to 8 inches apart after the last frost. Where montebretia isn't hardy, mulch it for the winter, or dig and store the corms in dry peat moss or other material. Propagate by division in the spring or fall, or by seed in the spring.

Some species and hybrids of *Tritonia* are also called montebretia and bear a strong resemblance to *Crocosmia*. See page 90.

Crocosmia × crocosmiiflora

Montebretia (*Crocosmia × crocosmiiflora*) was more popular in the past than it is today. It naturalizes readily and lasts for generations, so some older gardens have very large clumps that have spread far beyond their original boundaries.

Crocus

Iris family.
Corm; deciduous.
Blooms in winter, spring, or fall,
depending on species.

Location: Rock garden, meadow,
border, woodland, container, house
(seasonally), alpine house.

Soil: Well drained, sandy, acid to
neutral.

Care: Water regularly during season
of growth and flowering. Little or no
feeding is necessary.

Exposure: Sun or some light shade.

Famous as har-
bingers of
spring, crocuses
actually bloom
over much of the
year. The latest autumn-
blooming ones (not to be confused
with the misleadingly named autumn
crocus, *Colchicum*, page 50) bloom
nearly to the time when the first of
the spring crocuses begin. Crocuses
are native to the Mediterranean area,
but most crocuses sold today are
Dutch garden hybrids.

Flowers of crocuses are 2 to 4
inches tall, cup shaped or flaring.
They grow directly out of the
ground. Colors range from white to
blue, purple, lavender, orange, yellow, and gold. Some flowers are bicolored. The flowers close on cool,
dark days. Grasslike leaves with a
white central vein appear either before, with, or after the flowers, depending on the species; in most
Dutch garden varieties, which are
spring blooming, leaves appear before
or with the flowers. Where well
adapted, most types naturalize freely.
Spring-blooming crocuses force easily; see page 20.

Plant Dutch garden crocuses and
other spring-blooming types in the
fall, and fall-blooming types in late
summer. Set corms 5 inches deep
and 2 to 3 inches apart in the garden,
or 1 inch deep in a pot, seven to nine
per 5-inch pot. Most hybrids are
hardy to −40° F, with protected exposure and mulching. Crocus corms are
particularly vulnerable to rodents
such as voles and gophers.

Besides the large-flowered, vigorous Dutch garden crocuses, try some
of the smaller, subtler species. Here
are a few of the multitude of spring-
blooming species.

C. ancyrensis, from Turkey, bears
orange or golden yellow flowers,
sometimes with a brown base, in late
winter. 'Golden Bunch' flowers pro-
lifically. With good drainage it tolerates water during dormancy.

Dutch garden crocus 'Early Perfection'

C. biflorus (Scotch crocus), from
south-central Europe to Asia Minor,
in late winter has white or blue flowers striped purple, often with a
golden center. There are other color
forms. It demands dryness during
summer dormancy.

C. chrysanthus, a popular early species, has numerous named color
forms, from silvery blue to yellow,
orange yellow, deep purple, bright
blue, and white, most variously
marked. It is native from Bulgaria
through Asia Minor. It tolerates water during dormancy.

C. flavus, native from Yugoslavia
to Turkey, bears large golden yellow
to orange flowers in late winter or
early spring. It is very popular and
widely available.

C. imperati, from the mountains
near Naples, produces buff yellow
buds, feathered reddish violet and
opening to bright lilac in the winter
or early spring. It tolerates water
during dormancy.

C. sieberi, from Crete and Greece,
is rich lilac with a yellow center.
Various other color forms are sold;
one is banded lilac, white, and golden
yellow. It tolerates water during
dormancy.

C. tomasinianus, from Yugoslavia,
has starlike, bright lavender blossoms. It is usually hardy and adaptable, and it needs year-round
moisture.

C. vernus (Dutch crocus), from the
alpine regions of central and southern Europe, is the diminutive and
variable parent of the Dutch garden
hybrids. Some botanists consider it
an aggregate of several species. It
needs year-round moisture.

Here are some autumn- or early-
winter-blooming crocuses that are
widely sold. All are hardy to −30° F.

C. asturicus, from the mountains
of northern Spain, in early fall produces leaves, then flowers that are
mauve to violet with bright yellow
styles and anthers.

C. kotschyanus (*C. zonatus*), an alpine native from Turkey to Lebanon,
bears rose-lilac flowers with darker
veins and yellow centers in early fall.
It needs year-round moisture.

C. laevigatus 'Fontenayi', an early-
winter bloomer from Greece, has
wide-open rose-lilac, purple-
feathered flowers with the fragrance
of freesia. It prefers dryness during
dormancy.

C. sativus (*saffron crocus*) in fall
bears large, fragrant purple flowers.
Their red stigmas yield the spice
saffron.

C. speciosus, a variable species from
southeastern Europe to Iran, has numerous named varieties. It is the
earliest of fall-flowering crocuses.
This species needs year-round
moisture.

*Crocus
vernus*

Cyclamen hederifolium

Cyclamen persicum

Cyclamen

Primrose family.
Tuber; deciduous.
Blooms continuously fall into spring
(C. *persicum* hybrids), or for shorter
periods during these seasons
(species).

Florist's cyclamen *(C. persicum)*

Location: House, greenhouse, container, border.

Soil: Well drained, organic, neutral to alkaline.

Care: Water regularly but not excessively and feed regularly with a weak complete fertilizer during growth and blooming; dry off (but not completely) during spring and summer, after blooming ends. Store in dark place in pot.

Exposure: Filtered sunlight, perhaps from an east-facing window.

Florist's cyclamen, a group of 8- to 12-inch-tall hybrids of C. *persicum*, bears white, purple, red, pink, rose, salmon, or bicolored shooting-star flowers and attractive, mottled heart-shaped leaves. It can grow outdoors where temperatures do not drop below 20° F, but is more widely grown as a houseplant. The tubers are not offered for sale, only potted plants. Many forms, including dwarfs, are available.

The secret to success in maintaining florist's cyclamen is a humid, cool environment. A room that is 60° to 65° F during the day and 40° to 50° F at night is suitable. Repot during dormancy, with the tuber at the surface, and keep soil just barely moist until fall sprouting begins. Propagate by division of tubers, or by sowing seeds.

Hardy cyclamen

Location: Rock garden, woodland, border, container.

Soil: Well drained, neutral to alkaline.

Care: Water during period of growth and blooming. No feeding is necessary in most garden soils.

Exposure: Light shade.

Far hardier but smaller and more delicate than florist's cyclamen, the various species provide intri- cately marked foliage and masses of exceptionally graceful flowers to brighten the garden during its least colorful seasons. Marbled leaves, often with red undersides, appear before or after flowering, depending on species. Planted beneath shrubs, around trees, in mixed borders, rock gardens, lightly shaded wild gardens, or containers, the species cyclamen are among the most highly prized flowers of experienced gardeners.

Plant the tubers ½ inch deep and 6 to 8 inches apart during their dormant period. Most withstand some summer rain if the soil drains quickly. In areas with very cold winters or wet summers, alpine-house conditions are recommended. Propagate by division of tubers, or with fresh seeds, which germinate at the same time that leaves appear on mature plants of the same species. Cover seeds with soil at 55° to 60° F.

Cyclamen are most vigorous where they receive at least a hard frost during winter. Among the hardier species are the following.

C. *coum*, from the Caucasus, bears white to pink or crimson flowers, winter to early spring. Hardy to –20° F.

C. *hederifolium* (C. *neapolitanum*), from southern Europe to Asia Minor, bears pink or white flowers with dark eyes, in late summer and fall. Petals are sometimes gracefully twisted. Hardy to –20° F.

C. *pseudibericum*, from Asia Minor, bears striking crimson carmine or purplish flowers with white-bordered reddish purple blotches from winter to spring. Hardy to –10° F.

C. *purpurascens* (C. *europaeum*), from the European Alps, bears heavily scented rose red or rose pink to magenta flowers with crimson blotches on their bases, in late summer to fall. Hardy to –20° F.

Cyclamen pseudibericum

Cyrtanthus purpureus

Cyrtanthus purpureus

(Vallota speciosa)
Scarborough lily

Amaryllis family.
True bulb; evergreen or deciduous, depending on growing conditions. Blooms in late summer or early autumn.

Location: Bed, container, greenhouse, house.

Soil: Well drained, sandy, acid to neutral.

Care: Water regularly and give frequent, light feedings with complete fertilizer during spring growth period; during winter, reduce watering and stop feeding.

Exposure: Sun or light shade.

Since around 1800, when some bulbs of this South African flower washed ashore from a shipwreck at Scarborough, England, the Scarborough lily has been cultivated mainly as a houseplant for its umbels of brilliant scarlet flowers. Each 1½- to 2-foot stalk bears 6 to 9 flowers 2½ inches wide, above a fan of handsome straplike leaves. It can be planted outside only in frost-free areas. It is widely sold by specialists and a few general suppliers.

Plant the bulbs 2 or 3 inches deep in the garden or in pots, with the tips of the bulbs barely covered. Scarborough lily blooms best when it's rootbound, so plant the bulbs in small pots and repot them only when they become crowded. Bulbs in the garden tend not to bloom the first year and resent disturbance. Propagate in the early summer, before the blooming period, by careful separation of offsets from the parent bulb.

Specialists sometimes offer other *Cyrtanthus* species, most of them bearing umbels of tubular flowers.

Cyrtanthus purpureus

Cactus-flowered dahlia 'Match'

Dahlia

Composite family.
Tuberous root; deciduous.
Blooms from early summer to fall.

Location: Border, container.

Soil: Deep, well drained, sandy, organic, acid to neutral.

Care: Water regularly and feed with a low-nitrogen fertilizer during the growing season. Where winter temperatures drop below 10° F, dry off, dig, and store clumps or individual tubers in dry, cool medium over winter.

Exposure: Sun; some midday shade in hottest areas.

From a couple of Mexican wildflowers, hybridists have created a staggering array of extravagantly showy garden plants ranging in height from about 1 foot to 7 feet and bearing button-sized to dinnerplate-sized flowers in a huge assortment of forms and colors. They can be grown anywhere in the United States. Perhaps more than any other flower, dahlias offer the perfect solution to the gardener's problem of how, without intricate planning or hard labor, to have lots of bright color in the garden throughout the summer until the first frost. They provide serviceable cut flowers lasting up to a week.

You can plant seeds or seedlings of dwarf types (seedlings are available from nurseries) directly in garden soil as soon as it is warm. Space them 12 to 18 inches apart. Plant the seeds of large types indoors in early spring, then transplant the seedlings when the danger of frost has passed. It is more usual to plant tuberous roots, setting them horizontally beneath 3 inches of deeply prepared soil. As shoots grow, fill in with 1 to 3 inches more soil. Drive stakes into place when you set out tuberous roots of larger-growing varieties, to avoid injuring roots later. Pinch shoot tips twice to encourage fullness, first after two or three sets of leaves have developed, and again in a few weeks. As taller varieties grow, tie them to their stakes with cloth or other soft material. Watch for signs of mildew and spray with triforine if it appears. If you dig and store the tuberous roots in the fall, be careful not to break or cut them unnecessarily. Do not wash them. Dry them for a day, sprinkle bulb dust on the damaged surfaces, and store them in shallow trays in a dry medium. In the spring, separate the roots by dividing clumps for propagation purposes. Each division should include some of the old stem.

To help you read current catalogs, here are two lists of standard dahlia classifications—the first is by flower size; the second by flower form. The second list includes only the more popular flower types.

Flower Size Classification

AA (Giant): over 10 inches in diameter
A (Large): 8 to 10 inches in diameter
B (Medium): 6 to 8 inches in diameter
BB (Small): 4 to 6 inches in diameter
M (Miniature): up to 4 inches in diameter

Flower Form Classification

Anemone: One or more rows of petals surrounding a dense group of tubular florets.
Ball: Double blooms that are rounded or slightly flattened on top, with spirals arranged in petals.
Cactus-flowered: Double blooms with many petals, showing no disc; may be incurved toward center, straight, or recurved outward from center.
Collarette: Outer circle of petals surrounding an inner circle of shorter petals.
Formal decorative: Double flowers with symmetrically shaped and arranged petals.
Informal decorative: Double flowers with long, unevenly spaced, often twisted petals.
Mignon: Plants about 12 to 18 inches tall with single flowers less than 2 inches in diameter.
Miniature: Flowers in shape of other dahlia forms, but on small plants.
Orchid: Star-shaped, open-centered single flowers with petals that curve backward at the ends.
Pompon: Miniature, more globular versions of the ball form.
Peony: Flowers with open centers surrounded by two or more rows of petals that may be curled or twisted.
Single: Flowers with open centers surrounded by a single row of petals that radiate outward.
Water lily: Flat double flowers with large, broad, sparse petals.

Dichelostemma

See *Brodiaea*, page 45.

Miniature Ball dahlia 'Crimson Royal'

Mignon dahlia 'Little Drummer Boy'

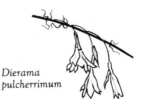

Dahlia hybrid   *Dierama pulcherrimum*

Dierama pulcherrimum

Dierama

Wand Flower, Fairy Wand, Angel's Fishing Rod

Iris family.
Corm; evergreen.
Blooms late summer, sometimes much earlier in mild-winter areas.

Location: Border, greenhouse.

Soil: Moist, organic, acid to neutral, with reasonable drainage.

Care: During growing season, water generously and feed occasionally with a complete fertilizer; never allow to dry completely.

Exposure: Sun.

One of the most arrestingly graceful of plants, wand flower bears nodding white, pink, rose, red, or maroon bell-shaped blossoms to 1½ inches long, encased in silvery bracts, on arching stems as much as 6 feet long. The delicate-looking but strong stems are thin as wire, and the leaves are also elegantly wiry. Plant this African native in the garden where most of the plant is visible, perhaps near a pool or against a hedge or other dark backdrop.

In spring set the corms 3 to 5 inches deep and a foot apart outside where the temperatures stay above 0° F, or put several corms in a large pot for cool greenhouse or alpine-house culture. Divide no more often than necessary, because corms take two to three years to recover to satisfactory flowering. Mulch after flowering. You can grow wand flower from seed in spring by covering seed slightly in a moist, bright spot where soil or medium is 60° to 65° F; germination takes one to six months.

D. pendulum, which is difficult to obtain, and *D. pulcherrimum,* which is sold by specialists, are quite similar; the latter has slightly larger flowers.

Dietes iridoides

Dietes

Butterfly iris, Fortnight lily

Iris family.
Rhizome; evergreen.
Blooms spring through fall, even into winter.

Location: Border, greenhouse.

Soil: Any well-drained garden soil.

Care: Very drought-tolerant once established, but water regularly and occasionally feed lightly with a complete fertilizer for best blooming.

Exposure: Sun or very light shade.

 Where winter temperatures do not drop below 20° F, this clumping South African native withstands gross neglect, maintaining its attractive, flat, grasslike foliage all year and producing waves of irislike blossoms over a season spanning most of the calendar. Both species are sold in pots or cans at general nurseries and can be planted in any season, though spring and fall are best. Individual flowers last only a day, but the plants bloom heavily for about two weeks, then rest for about two weeks—therefore the name, "fortnight lily." Divide them when they become crowded. They are easily propagated by division or seed.

D. bicolor (*Moraea bicolor*) grows to 2½ feet tall and bears 2-inch yellow flowers with blackish brown blotches. It is sometimes hard to find.

D. iridoides (*D. vegeta, Moraea vegeta, M. iridoides*) is widely available in warm-climate areas. It grows 3

Dietes grandiflora

Eranthis hyemalis

or 4 feet tall, with 3-inch, white, yellow-marked and blue-crested flowers. After a wave or an entire season of blooming, do not remove bloom stems, which produce flowers repeatedly. 'Johnsonii', which has 4-inch flowers and longer leaves, is occasionally available.

Endymion

See *Hyacinthoides*, page 71.

Eranthis

Winter aconite

Buttercup family.
Tuber; deciduous.
Blooms winter or early spring.

Location: Border, rock garden, woodland.

Soil: Well drained, organic, neutral to alkaline.

Care: Provide year-round moisture, particularly during growing period and summer. No feeding is necessary.

Exposure: Sun or partial shade.

 Usually the earliest bulb—blooming even before the first crocus—winter aconite, in drifts or clumps, breaks the somber mood of winter by paving the garden in sunshine yellow almost overnight. Each stem is topped by an upward-facing buttercuplike flower sitting on a ruff of foliage. It needs winter temperatures at least as low as 20° F, and is hardy to –30° F. Where well adapted it naturalizes by seeding itself, com-

ing to look as much at home in a wooded garden as in the woodlands of its native Europe and Asia. Virtually every supplier sells this bulb.

Plant tubers promptly upon receiving them, in late summer or early fall. Soak dry tubers for a few hours before setting them 5 inches deep and 1 to 2 inches apart. Handle the brittle tubers with care. Propagate by seeds, or by dividing clumps into smaller clumps.

Most commonly sold is *E. hyemalis*, 2 to 6 inches tall with 1-inch flowers. *E. cilicica*, to 2½ inches tall, is similar. *E. × tubergenii* is larger (2 to 8 inches) and slightly later than the others that are its parents; 'Guinea Gold' is fragrant.

Eremurus

Desert Candle, Foxtail lily

Lily family.
Tuberous root; deciduous.
Blooms late spring or early summer.

Location: Border.

Soil: Well drained, organic, sandy, acid to neutral.

Care: Give ample water during growing season. No feeding is necessary in most garden soils.

Exposure: Sun.

 Spikes from 3 to 7 feet tall above clumps of yuccalike leaves make eremurus one of the most distinctive and useful of border plants. Hundreds of small, lilylike, white or pastel flowers—and above the flowers, buds—cover the upper half of each tapered spike. Eremurus is a superb cut flower as well, lasting in the vase more than a week. Hybrids and several species are widely sold by specialists and some general suppliers.

Plant the clump of tuberous roots in early fall, taking care not to injure them. In a 2-foot hole, carefully spread the clump so the crown rests

Eranthis hyemalis

Eremurus

Erythronium californicum

on a central mound of sandy soil. When the hole is filled, the crown should be 4 to 6 inches deep. Do not disturb the plants unnecessarily. The foliage dies in the summer, so mark the positions of plants with stakes to avoid injuring them when you dig in the border. Propagate by sowing seeds, or by carefully lifting and dividing old plants when their crowns grow up out of the soil.

Most commonly grown are the Shelford and Ruiter hybrids, in a range of colors from white to pink, yellow, orange, and cream. The following species are also widely sold.

E. stenophyllus (*E. bungei*), from southwestern Asia, bears 2- to 3-foot spikes of yellow or golden yellow flowers.

E. himalaicus, from the Himalayas, grows to 4 feet tall and has white flowers.

E. robustus sometimes grows 8 to 10 feet but is usually around 6 feet tall and has bright, deep pink flowers. It is native to Turkestan.

Eremurus robustus

Erythronium americanum

Erythronium

Dog-tooth violet, Trout lily, Fawn lily

Lily family.
Corm; deciduous.
Blooms in spring.

Location: Woodland, border, rock garden.

Soil: Well drained, organic, acid to neutral.

Care: Water generously during period of growth and blooming, reduce watering afterward; no feeding is necessary in most garden soils.

Exposure: Light to medium shade.

Flowers and leaves of exceptional beauty distinguish the erythroniums. All of the species native to North American woodlands and meadows and the European and Asian species are similar in form, with one to several gracefully nodding lily flowers per plant, several bloom stems enclosed by pairs of folded, sometimes arching, often beautifully mottled leaves. Flower colors vary from white to cream, yellow, pink, and purple. Many species are hardy to –40° F, and all grow best where the ground freezes during the winter.

Plant corms as early as possible in the fall, 4 or 5 inches deep and 3 to 5 inches apart. Mulch to conserve moisture. Move the plants only when they become crowded. Propagate in July by sowing seeds uncovered in the shade.

The following species and one hybrid are splendid garden plants.

E. americanum, native to an area from Minnesota to Nova Scotia and Florida, grows to 2 feet and has yellow flowers, often spotted at their bases, and mottled leaves.

E. californicum, native to northern California and Oregon; grows from 4 to 14 inches tall; bears cream to white flowers with greenish yellow bases, banded inside with yellow, brown, or orange; and has mottled leaves.

E. dens-canis, from Europe and Asia, is a variable species bearing white or rose to purple, blue-anthered flowers and heavily mottled leaves. It is 6 to 12 inches tall.

E. helenae, native to northern California, grows up to 1 foot tall and has heavily mottled leaves and fragrant white and chrome yellow flowers.

E. hendersonii, from northern California and Oregon, has mottled leaves with crisped edges and lavender flowers with purple bases surrounded by yellow. It grows up to 1 foot tall.

E. × 'Pagoda', to 7 or 8 inches tall, has sulphur yellow flowers with a brown ring in the center and mottled leaves.

E. revolutum, native from British Columbia to California, has crisped, mottled leaves and rose-pink flowers with yellow bands on the inside bases of petals. 'White Beauty' has white flowers with yellow centers.

E. tuolumnense, from central California, grows to 18 inches tall and has golden yellow flowers with greenish centers.

Eucharis grandiflora

Eucharis grandiflora

(E. amazonica)
Amazon lily

Amaryllis family.
True bulb; evergreen.
Blooms in any season but most
heavily in late fall into spring.

Location: House, greenhouse, woodland in frost-free areas.

Soil: Acid to neutral, rich, organic.

Care: Water and feed heavily during
active growth; stop feeding and reduce watering at other times.

Exposure: Bright shade.

From the floor
of the tropical
Andean forests
comes this ex-
traordinarily beau-
tiful plant whose loose
umbels of nodding daffodillike, 3- to
4-inch-wide blossoms, three to six
per 18- to 24-inch stem, fill the house
or greenhouse with fragrance. With
mulching and some shade it grows
outside in southern Florida gardens.
Indoors it flowers at intervals
throughout the year if you meet
its needs.

Amazon lily is among the choicest
of cut flowers because of its beauty,
fragrance, and long vase life.

Early spring is the best planting
time, though any season is acceptable. In the garden, plant bulbs 3 to 4
inches deep, but in pots plant them
with the necks exposed. Space them
4 inches apart, or plant three or four
per 8-inch pot. Provide a constantly
humid atmosphere. To induce flowering, maintain a temperature of
80° F for four weeks, then lower the
temperature 10° F for 12 weeks. During the period of reduced temperature, reduce watering and apply no
fertilizer. After blooming, repeat the
cycle to induce reblooming.

*Eucharis
grandiflora*

*Eucomis
bicolor*

Eucomis comosa

Eucomis

Pineapple lily

Lily family.
True bulb; deciduous.
Blooms in summer, sometimes other
seasons.

Location: Border, container, greenhouse, house.

Soil: Well drained, sandy, organic,
acid to neutral.

Care: Water generously and feed
lightly with complete fertilizer during
growth and blooming. Reduce watering during dormancy, but do not dry
out completely.

Exposure: Sun or light shade.

Pineapplelike in
the way a tuft
of small leaves
crowns the
dense spike of
blooms (the "pine-
apple"), eucomis is easy to grow indoors or where temperatures stay

above 10° F in the garden. Its
straplike basal leaves are broad; the
leaves of some species have wavy or
crisped edges and are attractive for
several months each year. You can
buy this South African native from
some general suppliers as well as
from specialists. The spikes are excellent as cut flowers.

Plant the bulbs in March with
their necks barely exposed. Once
growth begins, start regular watering
and feeding. Grow in a humid atmosphere. You can alternate periods of
wetness and dryness to induce repeat
blooming. Propagate from offsets.

E. autumnalis (*E. undulata*) grows
to 20 inches tall and has wavy-edged
leaves and green flowers.

E. bicolor grows to 2½ feet high
and has crisped leaves and purple-
edged pale green flowers.

E. comosa grows to 2 feet tall and
has leaves with purple-spotted undersides and green, white, pinkish, or
purplish flowers. This species is especially good for cutting.

Ferraria crispa

Ferraria crispa

(F. undulata)

Iris family.
Corm; deciduous.
Blooms late spring, early summer.

Location: Greenhouse, alpine house, container, border.

Soil: Fast-draining, sandy, organic, acid to neutral.

Care: Water generously and feed lightly with complete fertilizer during period of growth and blooming; drying off during summer dormancy, though with fast drainage it usually tolerates summer rain.

Exposure: Sun, or some light shade in hot climates.

 Subtly similar to its more widely grown and more glamorous cousin, *Tigridia, Ferraria crispa* is the first of a fascinating and beautiful African genus to be occasionally offered to American gardeners by bulb specialists. It grows outdoors where temperatures don't drop below 0° F; elsewhere it makes an excellent container or seasonal garden plant whose corm can be dried off in its container, or dug and stored at 60° F in a packing medium. Its ¾-inch to 1½-inch flowers with heavily crisped petals are borne on stems up to 18 inches tall, above swordlike leaves. Flowers are curiously orchidlike and variably colored. Each flower lasts only one day, but new ones open with regularity.

In the garden, plant corms in spring as soon as daytime temperatures reach the fifties or sixties and nighttime temperatures stay around 40° F. Plant them 3 to 4 inches deep, 6 to 8 inches apart. Indoors plant them in late winter, 1 inch deep. During the growing season, feed lightly several times.

Ferraria crispa

Freesia refracta

Freesia hybrids

Freesia

Iris family.
Corm; deciduous.
Blooms in spring.

Location: Border, rock garden, container, alpine house, greenhouse, house.

Soil: Well drained, sandy, acid to neutral.

Care: Water regularly and feed very lightly during period of growth and flowering. Dry off during summer dormancy in hot areas. (In the far north, it is a summer grower.) Store in pots or uncovered in wet-summer areas.

Exposure: Sun or very light shade.

 Freesia, a native of South Africa, bears elegant flowers on slender, gracefully angled, tapering spikes above fans of miniature gladioluslike leaves. It also has one of the most beautiful flower fragrances. The flaring, trumpet-shaped flowers, to 2 inches long, are white or shades of yellow, gold, orange, pink, red, purple, or violet. Many are bicolored and beautifully veined or feathered. Some are double. Species grow 10 to 12 inches high, sometimes higher, and the hybrids grow to 18 inches. In gardens where the temperature doesn't drop below 20° F, and where the summers are dry and the winters cool and moist, freesias are perennial. Elsewhere they must be grown under cool alpine-house conditions. They are easily forced indoors (see page 19) and are one of the best cut flowers, lasting 5 to 12 days and filling the room with their fragrance.

In the South, plant corms in the garden in the fall, pointed ends up, 2 inches deep, and 1 or 2 inches apart or 1 inch deep in pots, six to eight per 6-inch pot. In the North, plant them in the spring. You can stagger plantings for blooming 10 to 12 weeks after planting. Water during the growing period, but don't overwater. Freesias tend to sprawl, so plant them close together for support and provide additional support if it is needed. Propagate from offsets.

Most of the available freesias are hybrids, usually named varieties or groups. Occasionally you may find *F. refracta*, which has extremely fragrant greenish yellow flowers marked with brownish yellow and purple; there is also a white form. Or you may find *F. alba*, which is white marked with yellow.

Fritillaria imperialis

Fritillaria

Fritillary

Lily family.
True bulb; deciduous.
Blooms in spring.

Location: Border, rock garden, meadow, woodland, container, alpine house.

Soil: Well drained. For most species, organic, nearly neutral.

Care: For most species, water regularly and reduce water when plants die back after blooming; feed regularly with complete fertilizer in early spring.

Exposure: Sun or light shade, depending on species.

From one of the most imposing border flowers to subtler, sometimes diminutive plants for rock garden, meadow, or woodland, this diverse genus from various parts of the Northern Hemisphere has long been prized by bulb fanciers. All have bell- or cuplike flowers, usually nodding, with a shiny reservoir of nectar near the inner base of each petal. The species described here are occasionally to readily available and are widely adapted. Included are a few less-known, more challenging fritillarias whose cultural requirements deviate from those described above.

Plant in late summer or very early fall, 4 to 8 inches deep and 2 to 12 inches apart, depending on the size of the bulbs. Do not allow the bulbs to

Fritillaria pluriflora

dry out by leaving them unplanted for any length of time, and be careful not to damage their vulnerable fleshy scales. Propagate by division in the fall, or (some species) by bulb cuttings, placing individual scales in moist sand.

F. camschatcensis (Kamchatka lily), native from Japan to Alaska and southward, produces a stem 1 to 2 feet tall, surrounded by whorls of leaves, and bearing one to six dark purplish chocolate bells. It is very hardy and prefers cool-summer climates, some shade, and rich, moist, acid soil. It is sometimes offered by specialists.

F. imperialis (crown imperial), the largest and most widely grown fritillaria, is native to India, Afghanistan, and Iran. Atop a 2- to 4-foot stem with whorls of glossy leaves is a cluster of nodding orange, red, or yellow flowers capped by a dense tuft of smaller leaves. It is best when allowed to form large clumps in sunny borders. It sometimes needs staking, and some people object to its musky odor. This species grows best in cold-winter areas.

F. lanceolata (checker lily or mission bells) is native from British Co-

lumbia to California and eastward to Idaho. It grows from 1 to nearly 3 feet tall and bears brownish purple to greenish yellow flowers. It prefers light shade and, unlike many other West Coast native fritillarias, tolerates some summer watering. A few specialists offer it.

F. latifolia, an old-fashioned garden favorite now seldom sold, is native to the Caucasus. It grows to 1 foot tall and bears grayish leaves and large, deep brown flowers prominently checkered yellow or greenish.

F. meleagris, the widely sold checkered lily (also called snake's head and guinea-hen tulip) from Europe, bears one to three bell-shaped, extravagantly checkered and veined flowers varying from deep brown to rose lilac and wine, even white. It is suited to borders, meadows, and bright woodlands—anywhere the soil is rich and moist—and it grows best in cold-winter areas.

F. pallidiflora, another very hardy species, is from the mountainous areas of Siberia. It bears two or three nodding creamy to greenish yellow, tuliplike flowers checkered red or brown, atop a 9- to 15-inch stem. Some specialists sell it.

Galanthus nivalis

F. persica, from Iran, produces up to 30 deep violet to deep reddish purple or straw-colored blossoms on a 2- to 3-foot stem. Variety 'Adiyama' has especially fine deep plum-purple flowers. *F. persica* is suitable for borders in cool-climate areas. It is often sold by specialists.

F. pluriflora, from northern California, is a perfect rock garden or alpine-house plant. On 6- to 16-inch stems it bears one to seven large, pendulous, pink to rose blossoms. It likes sun or light shade, mild winters, and light, fast-draining soil. Dry it off after blooming ends. It is sold by a few specialists.

F. pontica, from southeast Europe and Asia Minor, grows in light shade. On 8- to 18-inch stems it has one to three green flowers with purplish brown tips. Some specialists sell it.

F. roderickii (F. grayana), native to the Pacific headlands in northern California, bears one to three nodding, brown or greenish brown, bell-like flowers with a whitish area on each petal. It fares best in a cool-summer, mild-winter rock garden or meadow or in an alpine house. After blooming it requires drying off until mid- to late fall. This species is rarely sold commercially.

Fritillaria imperialis

Galanthus plicatus × nivalis

Galanthus

Snowdrop

Amaryllis family.
True bulb; deciduous.
Blooms late winter to early spring.

Location: Mixed border, meadow, woodland, rock garden, container seasonally indoors.

Soil: Cool, moist, heavy or organic, neutral to alkaline.

Care: Water regularly and generously through bloom period; little fertilizing is needed.

Exposure: Light shade.

Along with winter aconite, snowdrop is one of the first flowers of the season, often blooming out of melting snow and undisturbed by further snowfall. In mass plantings it brings delicate beauty and fragrance to winter-drab landscapes. Native to the deciduous woodlands of Europe and Asia Minor, the species discussed here thrive and naturalize if you can approximate cool woodland conditions where winter low temperatures reach at least 20° F, but not colder than –30° F. Sweeping drifts of bulbs can last for decades. Indoors, too, snowdrop can brighten the winter if you start bulbs 1 inch deep, about four per 4-inch pot, in a frame or unheated greenhouse in the fall, then bring them to a very cool, bright

indoor spot as buds begin to develop. Or you can lift clumps in early winter, transfer them to containers, and move them to a cool, bright indoor spot.

In the garden plant bulbs 3 to 4 inches deep and 2 to 3 inches apart in the fall. Propagate snowdrop by dividing the clumps immediately after flowering into sections of no fewer than four or five bulbs. Replant immediately. Or sow the seeds in June in pans of moist potting medium, and transplant the seedlings a year later.

G. elwesii (giant snowdrop) grows 6 to 12 inches tall and bears nodding 1½ inch flowers whose rounded outer petals are pure white and whose three smaller, inner petals are marked with green. Native to Asia Minor, *G. elwesii* withstands hot weather better than *G. nivalis.*

G. nivalis bears a strong similarity to its cousin but blooms a bit earlier and is smaller and daintier, with 1-inch flowers on 6-inch stems. Many varieties are sold. Among the choicest are 'Atkinsii', which is very early blooming, large blossomed, and adaptable; and 'Flore Pleno', which is double flowered. You may find these varieties more difficult to locate than the species.

You may occasionally find choice but rarely sold species like *G. byzantinus* and *G. plicatus.* All *Galanthus* species bear a close resemblance to each other.

Galaxia barnardii

Galaxia

Iris family.
Corm; deciduous.
Blooms in winter.

Location: Container, rock garden, alpine house.

Soil: Well drained, sandy, acid to neutral.

Care: Water regularly during growing season, through winter until the foliage withers, then dry off during dormancy.

Exposure: Sun.

From the Cape region of South Africa comes this little-known genus of crocuslike dwarf bulbs that lend themselves to cultivation in rock gardens where winters are mild and in containers elsewhere. During the winter they produce a rosette of nearly prostrate 2- or 3-inch leaves, just above which the apparently stemless flowers appear in bursts.

In the fall, plant corms 1 inch deep in the ground or in pots, six corms per 6-inch pot. Thorough drying off in baking heat is a key to success in growing galaxia. In frosty climates dig and store the corms in packing material after drying off. Propagate by seed or offsets in fall.

Most species have bright yellow flowers. G. citrina, G. fugacissima, and G. ovata have flowers about ¾-inch wide. G. grandiflora has 1½- to 2-inch-wide flowers.

G. barnardii has 1¼- to 1½-inch, pinkish purple flowers with nearly black centers.

G. versicolor bears ¾- to 1-inch flowers in shades of pink, red, or purple with yellow or dark red centers.

G. variabilis has 1- to 2-inch, pink, yellow, or white flowers with yellow centers.

Galaxis fugacissima

Galtonia candicans

Galtonia

Lily family.
True bulb; deciduous.
Blooms in summer.

Location: Border.

Soil: Well drained, sandy, organic, acid to neutral.

Care: Water regularly during growth and blooming; no feeding is necessary in most garden soils.

Exposure: Sun or light shade.

Fragrant galtonia bears up to 30 white or green-tinged, nodding flowers on each sturdy 2- to 4-foot spike, above 2- to 3-foot straplike leaves.

Galtonia candicans

This South African native, sold by a few specialists and general suppliers, deserves greater popularity as a choice border flower. It is also a first-rate cut flower that lasts more than a week. A hardy bulb, it grows with protection of heavy winter mulching in gardens that get as cold as –20° F. Elsewhere it must be dried off in fall, dug, and stored cool in a packing material.

Plant bulbs in fall or early spring, 6 to 9 inches deep. Protect against snails and slugs.

G. candicans (Hyacinthus candicans), called summer hyacinth, has white flowers with dark stamens.

Similar but slightly smaller is G. princeps (Hyacinthus princeps), whose flowers are sparser and greenish white.

Geissorhiza radians

Gladiolus callianthus

Geissorhiza

Iris family.
Corm; deciduous.
Blooms in spring and early summer.

Location: Rock garden, alpine house, container.

Soil: Well drained, sandy, acid to neutral, not too rich.

Care: Water after weather cools in autumn, through winter and spring, until after flowering; then dry out, dig, and store, until cool fall weather. No fertilizing is necessary in garden soil.

Exposure: Sun.

The beauty of geissorhiza is startling. Flowers of even the more subtle species are attractive, and the showier ones are so striking that, when a slide of G. *radians* was flashed on a screen before a group of horticultural society members, the response was an immediate, unified gasp. The flowers are a variety of bright colors, including bi- and tricolors. Plants are generally low growing and look like their close relatives ixia and hesperantha. The genus is seldom grown in the United States, but as corms and seed of this South African plant become more available, it will likely take its place in the collections of many gardeners. At present, it is rarely sold.

Plant corms outside where the temperature does not drop below 10° F, and in alpine houses or bulb frames elsewhere. Plant them in the early fall, 4 inches deep and 5 or 6 inches apart. Plants growing under glass can be transplanted into the garden after the danger of frost is past. After blooming, dry out, dig, and put the corms back to grow under glass. For culture in containers, plant four or five corms per 6-inch pot, burying them beneath 1 or 2 inches of soil. Propagate from cormlets or seeds.

Of the approximately 65 species, the following are among the most attractive, though any geissorhiza that you can locate is well worth growing.

G. *corrugata* is about 2 inches high and has corkscrew leaves and bright yellow flowers ½ inch wide.

G. *inflexa* and its variety *erosa* are 8 to 9 inches tall and have 1- to 1¼-inch flowers ranging from flesh-colored to rosy pink and glowing red.

G. *monantha* is 3 to 4 inches tall and has 1¼-inch-wide flowers that are intense purple with shiny white centers.

G. *radians* (G. *rochensis*) is 3 to 4 inches tall and has 1½-inch brilliant purple flowers whose bright red centers are bordered by a thin white line.

G. *splendidissima* is 3 to 4 inches tall and has ½- to ¾-inch flowers of darkest purple with bright green centers.

G. *tulbaghensis* is 3 inches tall and produces an abundance of 1- to 1¼-inch white flowers with pale mauve centers.

Geissorhiza aspera

Gladiolus

Iris family.
Corm; deciduous.
Blooms ordinarily in spring, summer, or fall, but in areas with mild winters and summers or in greenhouses, garden gladiolus can be planted any time to bloom 60 to 100 days later.

Garden Gladiolus and Summer-Growing Species

Location: Border, rock garden, alpine house, greenhouse, container.

Soil: Well drained, sandy, organic, acid to neutral.

Care: Water regularly during growth and blooming; then dry, dig, and store uncovered in well-ventilated, cool spot, or leave in place if climate permits. For garden varieties, mix bone meal or superphosphate thoroughly into planting soil beneath corms, and feed with 5–10–10 fertilizer a month after planting and again when spikes begin to develop.

Exposure: Sun.

A triumph of modern hybridization, garden gladiolus can provide color in astonishing variety and on a startlingly varied scale through as much of the year as your climate or your energy and growing facilities permit. Their colors include numerous bi- and tricolors—and even greens—but lack a true blue. Their size (from 1½ to 5 or 6 feet, with flowers up to 6 inches wide) and towering habit suit them to planting in clumps or larger masses. Try

Garden gladiolus
make some of the
most colorful and
dramatic additions
to the summer gar-
den. Because they
do not need winter
chilling to bloom,
corms can be
planted throughout
the summer for a
succession of
blooms. Plant
about 10 weeks
before you want
them to bloom.
These are 'Priscilla'
(white) and 'Com-
mando' (red).

Gloriosa rothschildiana

just one variety per grouping, larger types at the back of a border or among low-growing shrubs, rather than lined up regimentally (unless they are in a cutting garden). Miniature hybrids and diminutive species provide for the rock garden, border, or containers various colors that are subtler, for the most part, and forms that are looser and less rigid. All gladiolus make long-lasting cut flowers, with a vase life of one to two weeks; cut a spike when its first flower has opened.

Plant corms 4 to 6 inches deep and 2 to 6 inches apart. In hot-summer areas, time the planting so that blooming will occur during cooler weather. In windy areas stake garden varieties as necessary (deep planting helps, too). Watch for signs of thrips (washed-out, streaked leaves and distorted flowers). See page 33. Dust stored corms thoroughly with malathion where thrips are a problem. Propagate from the new corm or the numerous cormlets that form.

In addition to the myriad garden varieties, there are two winter-dormant, summer-growing species that bloom in late summer or fall. They should be lifted and stored over winter except where winters are moderate; in fast-draining soil they usually tolerate winter rain. Feed them very lightly.

G. *callianthus*, widely sold as *Acidanthera bicolor* or *A. murieliae* and commonly called Abssyinian gladiolus, is native to eastern Africa. It grows to 3 feet tall and bears 10 to 12 very fragrant 4-inch white flowers blotched with chocolate or reddish purple.

G. *papilio* (G. *purpureo-auratus*), from South Africa, has grassy leaves and tall, slender stems bearing curiously hooded flowers varying from greenish to yellowish white, usually with an intricate mauve and cream blotch. It spreads by stolons. You may have difficulty locating a source.

Winter-Growing Species

Location: Rock garden, alpine house, container.

Soil: Well drained, sandy, acid to neutral.

Care: Water regularly during growth and blooming, late fall into spring, then dry off during summer dormancy. In wet-summer areas, dig and store like garden gladiolus or shelter in alpine house conditions. Feed lightly during growth and blooming.

Exposure: Sun.

Some splendid species from the dry-summer Cape Province of South Africa are perfectly suited to gardens of our western dry-summer, mild-winter areas and for alpine house cultivation elsewhere. The following are occasionally offered by some specialists.

G. *alatus* grows to 6 to 12 inches tall and bears three to five fragrant flowers per arching stem. Flowers are hooded, with three broad, spreading upper petals and three narrow, drooping lower ones. Petals vary from pink or orange to brick red, and lower petals are marked with pale yellow.

G. *carneus* (G. *blandus*) grows to 2 feet tall and bears 3 to 10 pale pink, purplish, or creamy flowers with pink or purplish markings on the lower petals, sometimes with a blotch at the center of each flower.

G. *tristis*, a rather widely sold species, has night-scented yellowish flowers, three to six per 1½- to 2-foot spike. There are several forms in various colors.

Gladiolus × *colvillei*

Gloriosa rothschildiana

Gloriosa

Gloriosa lily, Climbing lily

Lily family.
Tuber; deciduous vine.
Blooms outdoors late summer to fall; indoor bloom time depends on time of planting (usually spring for summer and fall blooming).

Location: House, greenhouse, outdoor bed where winters aren't colder than 10° F, or container seasonally.

Soil: Fast draining, organic, acid to neutral.

Care: Except after blooming and through dormancy, water and feed regularly with complete fertilizer.

Exposure: Light to medium shade.

Dramatically shaped yellow and red flowers, glossy tendril-tipped leaves, and a vining habit make this  South African member of the lily family one of the most unusual of bulbs. Its slender stem climbs four to eight feet and produces graceful 4- to 5-inch flowers.

If cut just before petals bend back, flowers last up to eight days. If you cut the main stem, split the cut end before putting it into a vase.

Plant the fingerlike tuber horizontally, 2 inches deep, outdoors after the last frost or indoors any season (spring is the best time) to take advantage of bright light and warm summer temperatures. This tropical vine prefers 60° to 70° F nights and at least 75° F daytime temperatures, together with high humidity; however, it tolerates night temperatures in the 50s. In an 8-inch pot, plant one to three rhizomes. For a long bloom period outdoors, start the tubers indoors in late winter, then transplant. After blooming, gradually cease watering, then dig and store the tubers dry for about six months at 55° to 60° F, or leave them in pots of dry soil until spring, then repot in fresh soil. Propagate during repotting by offsets or divisions of the rhizome, or sow seeds indoors in any season, after two months of chilling, with a constant 70° to 75° F soil temperature.

Widely available is G. *rothschildiana*, which has yellow-based and bordered, wavy-edged crimson petals. More difficult to locate is the variety 'Citrina', which is yellow brushed with purple.

Gloxinia

See *Sinningia*, page 86.

Habranthus robustus

Hemerocallis 'Valiant'

Habranthus

Amaryllis family.
True bulb; deciduous.
Blooms in summer.

Location: Border, rock garden, container, house, greenhouse.

Soil: Well drained, sandy, neutral to alkaline.

Care: Water regularly during spring and summer, then reduce watering, or dry off and store warm.

Exposure: Sun.

After summer rains this native of Texas and South America produces showy, funnel-shaped flowers directly out of the ground. Foliage appears before or with flowers. Both species listed below are sold occasionally by some specialists.

In the spring plant the bulbs in the garden 4 to 5 inches deep and 6 inches apart, or plant one bulb per 6-inch pot, with the top of the bulb exposed. Allow plants to become rootbound. Propagate from offsets in spring.

H. *tubispathus*, from South America and Texas, bears dark yellow flowers with copper red on the backs of the petals. Flowers height reaches 6 inches.

H. *robustus* (*Zephyranthes robustus*), from Argentina, bears rose-red or rosy pink, greenish-throated flowers 9 inches high.

Habranthus andersonii

Hemerocallis aurantiaca

Haemanthus katharinae

See *Scadoxus multiflorus ssp. katharinae*, page 85.

Hemerocallis

Daylily
Lily family.
Tuberous roots; deciduous or evergreen.
Blooms late spring to fall.

Location: Border.

Soil: Any well-drained garden soil, not too rich.

Care: Plants tolerate drought and neglect but bloom best with regular watering and occasional light feeding with a complete fertilizer.

Exposure: Sun or partial shade.

The widely sold hybrid daylilies offer beauty, variety, and versatility and make few demands on the gardener. Most of these descendants of plants from Europe and Asia—especially Japan—adapt throughout the United States, even in the coldest areas with winter mulching. Daylilies bear blossoms up to 5—or even 7—inches wide, in colors ranging from the yellow, orange, and tawny red of old-fashioned favorites, to a multitude of shades and bicolor combinations of cream, yellow, gold, red, pink, apricot, purple, violet, and plum. Gracefully arching 1- to 2-foot leaves rise from the bases of the plants and form mounds. The clusters of flowers are held above or near the upper edges of these mounds. The tallest varieties are up to 4 feet high, and the smallest ones only 1 foot. Daylilies can be massed as a large-scale ground cover, planted in perennial or mixed borders, or used as edging.

Blooming lasts about a month, and though individual flowers last only a day, they are borne profusely in an unbroken succession. By choosing varieties that bloom at different times, you can have daylily blossoms from late spring into fall. "Early" varieties bloom in late May or June, "midseason" varieties in July, and "late" ones in August or early September. Daylilies are useful as cut flowers. (To make blossoms open in the evening, refrigerate during the day.) Yellow varieties are often fragrant. For the tidiest effect in the vase or the garden, remove withered blossoms daily.

Plant tuberous roots or nursery plants anytime during the growing season, though spring or fall is best. Set crowns close to the surface of the soil, and space plants 1½ to 3 feet apart. Daylilies thrive in full sun—but in the hottest climates their flowers look best with some shade—or light to medium shade. They accept virtually any well-drained soil. Propagate by division.

Hermodactylus tuberosus

Hermodactylus tuberosus

(Iris tuberosa)
Snake's-head iris, Widow iris

Iris family.
Tuber; deciduous.
Blooms late winter or early spring.

Location: Rock garden, border, container, alpine house.

Soil: Well drained, neutral to alkaline.

Care: Water during active growth from fall until after blooming, then dry off. No fertilizing is necessary in good garden soil.

Exposure: Sun.

The very dark brownish purple falls and olive green standards of this 2-inch flower, which otherwise resembles Dutch iris, are subtle rather than showy. Native to rocky hillsides of the Mediterranean area, hermodactylus adapts in gardens that do not get colder than 10° F if it has fast drainage and a sheltered, sun-baked spot. In late winter or spring, long, narrow, thick leaves appear simultaneously with the 10- to 18-inch flower stems, each bearing one blossom. The old section of prostrate tuber dies after the new shoot appears, and a new section of tuber develops ahead of the shoot. So, hermodactylus moves through gardens and needs repotting yearly. In the garden, it should be undisturbed for several years.

Plant during dormancy, in late summer or early fall. Propagate by division. Sold by specialists.

Hermodactylus tuberosus

Hesperantha humilis

Hesperantha

Iris family.
Corm; deciduous.
Blooms in spring.

Location: Rock garden, alpine house, container.

Soil: Well drained, sandy, acid to neutral, not too rich.

Care: Water after weather cools in autumn, through winter and spring, until after flowering; then dry out, or dig and store, until cool fall weather. No fertilizing is necessary in good garden soil.

Exposure: Sun.

Native mostly to wet-winter areas of Africa south of the Sahara, hesperantha bears a close resemblance to its relatives ixia and geissorhiza. Unlike the relatives, however, many hesperantha species open their flowers in late afternoon, when the moths that pollinate them are out, and close them at night. Other species are day blooming. Where winter temperatures do not drop below 10° F, you can grow hesperantha outdoors the year around. Elsewhere, you can grow it under glass, or under glass and seasonally outdoors, like geissorhiza (see page 65). Propagate from cormlets or seed.

Among the evening-blooming species are *H. bachmanii (H. angusta)* and *H. cucullata (H. buhrii)*, both bearing sweet-scented white flowers on 1-foot spikes. The similar *H. falcata* has gleaming white flowers marked with red on the outside.

The following species are day blooming.

H. humilis, a miniature less than 3 inches tall, bears large rosy pink, darker-centered flowers.

H. pauciflora, to 10 inches tall, has pink to reddish purple flowers.

H. purpurea bears 10-inch stems of rich reddish purple, darker-based flowers, above 3-inch leaves.

H. vaginata, the most widely grown species, grows 7 inches or taller and has striking, rich golden yellow, 2-inch flowers whose petal tips and bases are usually marked with black. However, coloration is somewhat variable in this species. Flowers open in early afternoon for a few hours.

Hesperantha is available from specialists, though you may have difficulty obtaining particular species.

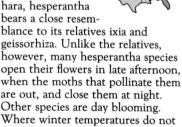

Hesperantha bachmanii

Hippeastrum

Amaryllis

Amaryllis family.
True bulb; deciduous.
Blooms indoors winter or spring;
outdoors, spring.

Location: Border, container, house,
greenhouse.

Soil: Well drained, organic, sandy,
slightly acid.

Care: Water initially during root
growth in winter, then water regularly after the sprout appears; dry
hippeastrums off after foliage withers, during summer and fall, but do
not let the bulbs shrivel. During the
growth period, water regularly (but
do not overwater), and feed 2 to 3
times a month with a complete fertilizer. Mix bone meal or superphosphate into potting soil.

Exposure: Full sun or light shade;
flowers last longer with some light
shade during blooming.

In spite of its
common name,
hippeastrum
should not be
confused with
Amaryllis belladonna, an
entirely different plant. The many
plants from which our modern hybrid hippeastrums are bred grow in
the Amazon basin. From two to six,
but usually four, huge flowers are
borne atop each 12- to 36-inch stalk.

Bold, straplike foliage develops
simultaneously with or after flowering. Large bulbs frequently produce
two bloom stalks in a season. The 8-
to 10-inch flowers are shades of red,
pink, salmon, orange, or white, and
many are bicolored and striped or
subtly shaded. The sudden emergence of stalks from the bulbs and
rapid, showy blooming lend drama as
well as architectural beauty to rooms
graced by this favorite potted flower.
Hippeastrum is a choice cut flower,
lasting five to seven days.

In the garden, plant the bulbs with
their bases about 8 inches deep and
at least 1 foot apart, in the fall or
spring. To bring into bloom indoors,
in late fall or winter plant one bulb
per 6-inch pot, with a third of the
bulb above the rim of the pot. Water
once, thoroughly, and place the pot
at room temperature (at least 70° F),
in sunlight. Time from planting to
blooming is five to eight weeks. Stagger the plantings for a long season of
flowers.

Homeria elegans

After flowering, carefully cut off
the bloom stem. Keep the pot in the
sun and be sure to continue watering
and feeding until foliage has withered. Then rest the bulb. One
method is to keep the bulb in the
pot, dry it off and store it for 8 to 10
weeks, then begin the cycle again.
Another method is to place the potted plant in a cool (55° F) growing
area for 8 to 10 weeks and continue
to water; afterward, begin the
cycle again.

Change the soil every two to four
years, and propagate by offsets when
repotting.

Hippeastrum bulbs are susceptible
to rot if overwatered. Watch for
mealybug, thrips, and mites in the
garden.

*Hippeastrum
vittatum*

Hippeastrum hybrids

Homeria

Iris family.
Corm; deciduous.
Blooms in early spring.

Cultural needs and garden uses are
the same as for closely related ixia.
See page 74.

Resembling its
relatives ixia
and, to a lesser
extent, tigridia,
homeria is a South
African plant whose
handsome flowers each last only a
day, but repeat profusely over several
weeks. Colors include yellows, oranges, mauves, and many handsomely
variegated combinations. Aside from
the fairly available species described
here, quite a few other choice ones
are worth searching for—for example, *H. spiralis*, a miniature with yel-
low-starred, deep salmon flowers.

H. flaccida (*H. collina*, *H.
breyniana*) has orange flowers on 12-
to 18-inch stems.

H. ochroleuca (*Moraea collina* var.
ochroleuca) is similar except for its
soft yellow flowers.

H. elegans (painted homeria) is
bright yellow, boldly splashed with
orange or orange and green on alternate petals, and one form has alternate petals of solid orange.

All homerias are poisonous
if eaten.

*Homeria
ochroleuca*

Hyacinthoides hispanica

Hyacinthus orientalis

Hymenocallis calathina

Hyacinthoides

Bluebell, Wood hyacinth
Lily family.
True bulb; deciduous.
Blooms in spring.
Location: Woodland, border, container, rock garden.
Soil: Well drained, organic, acid to neutral.
Care: Water regularly beginning in fall, during growth and flowering; reduce watering or dry off in summer. No feeding is necessary in most soils.
Exposure: Partial shade or sun.

Often mistakenly sold as scilla or endymion, hyacinthoides are among the most delightful of the hardy spring bulbs. These hyacinth relatives from the woodland of western Europe have loose, graceful spikes of bell-shaped blue, pink, and white blossoms and lend themselves to naturalizing in bold clumps and drifts, or to container culture.

Plant bulbs in the fall, 2 to 5 inches deep and 3 to 4 inches apart in the garden, or 1 inch deep in pots, six or seven per 6-inch pot. Propagate by division or offsets.

H. hispanica (*Endymion hispanicus, Scilla campanulata, Scilla hispanica*), Spanish bluebell, grows up to 15 inches high and bears blue to rose-purple flowers. There are white and pink forms.

H. italica (*Endymion italicus, Scilla italica*), Italian bluebell, bears fragrant lilac-blue flowers on 1-foot spikes. It is less available than the others, but very desirable.

H. non-scripta (*Endymion non-scriptus, Scilla non-scripta*), English bluebell, bears lilac-blue flowers on stems to 18 inches tall. White, blue, and pink forms are sold.

Hyacinthus orientalis

Garden hyacinth
Lily family.
True bulb; deciduous.
Blooms in spring in the garden, winter indoors.
Location: Border or bed, container, house, greenhouse.
Soil: Fast draining, organic, acid to neutral.
Care: Water generously during period of growth and blooming, late fall to spring. Indoors, water once thoroughly at planting; then keep moist through forcing period.
Exposure: Sun or light shade.

Its heavenly fragrance makes the hardy garden hyacinth a bulb favorite. It is one of the few bulbs whose regularity of form and size suits it to formal plantings. Medium-sized bulbs are even better for this purpose than the most expensive exhibition grade of bulbs. Hyacinth is also a superlative container plant that can easily be forced for winter bloom indoors in pots or special hyacinth glasses (see page 21). Even the smallest, least expensive grades of bulbs lend themselves to informal plantings and, where adapted, they endure in the garden for several years. In their first year their spikes are dense, but in subsequent years spikes are longer and looser. They are good cut flowers, lasting up to 6 days. Cut when at least half of their buds have opened.

In the garden plant bulbs 4 to 6 inches deep and 6 to 8 inches apart. In containers plant the bulbs even with pot rims, five per 6-inch pot.

H. orientalis var. *albulus* (Roman hyacinth), which is rather difficult to locate, is smaller and earlier than the species. Its flowers are white to light blue, borne in loose spikes.

Hyacinthoides hispanica

Hyacinthus orientalis

Hymenocallis

Spider lily, Sea daffodil
Amaryllis family.
True bulb; deciduous.
Blooms in summer.
Location: Border, container, greenhouse, house.
Soil: Well drained, organic, acid to neutral.
Care: Water copiously and feed regularly with complete fertilizer during period of active growth; then stop feeding and dry off, or dig and store.
Exposure: Sun or very light shade.

Umbels of heavily fragrant, intricately formed, daffodillike flowers and broad, straplike leaves that last all summer are the appealing features of this group of plants from the tropical and subtropical areas of the Americas. They are frequently marketed as *Ismene calathina*. You may also want to grow closely related, strikingly similar pancratiums, from the Mediterranean area. (See page 82.) All hymenocallis and pancratiums make excellent cut flowers, lasting a week or longer.

Plant bulbs 1 foot apart (or, in containers, one bulb per 8-inch pot, with tips just beneath the surface of the soil). In frost-free locations, you can either leave the bulbs in the ground if drainage is excellent or dig them before frost and store them in packing material at 60° to 70° F until spring. Container-grown plants should be dried off once foliage has died back and stored (perhaps with pots turned on their sides under a greenhouse bench). Propagate from offsets in the fall or from the large seeds in the spring, in a 60° F medium. Repot every two or three years.

The following easy-to-grow hymenocallis species are generally available.

H. amancaes, from Peru, grows 1½ to 2 feet tall and bears 3 to 6 bright yellow flowers with green-streaked bases.

H. × festalis is a white-flowered hybrid derived from, and quite similar to, *H. narcissiflora*, but with narrower petals.

H. narcissiflora (usually sold as *H. calathina* or *Ismene calathina*), the most reliably hardy and widely available hymenocallis, is a native of the Peruvian and Bolivian Andes. It bears four to six large white flowers with green shading atop a 2-foot stem. 'Sulphurea' is pale yellow; 'Advance' has particularly durable flowers; 'Sulphur Queen' has yellow-green flowers.

Ipheion uniflorum

(Triteleia uniflora, Brodiaea uniflora)
Spring starflower

Allium family.
True bulb; deciduous.
Blooms in spring.

Location: Border, meadow, woodland, rock garden, container, alpine house, house.

Soil: Most well-drained soils.

Care: Drought tolerant; no feeding is necessary in most soils.

Exposure: Sun or light shade.

Here is a bright-flowered, profuse bloomer that you can plant and enjoy with no further effort; wherever it adapts it tends to naturalize. This native of Argentina and Uruguay, hardy to –20° F, produces 1½-inch, blue-tinged white or blue flowers with bright orange stamens, one per 6- to 8-inch stem. Its leaves appear in the fall. It is widely available and adapts happily between flagstones, in chinks of walls—virtually anywhere in the garden.

Plant bulbs in the fall, 4 to 5 inches deep and 1 to 4 inches apart. In cold-winter areas, protect it with mulch.

Ipheion uniflorum

Hymenocallis narcissiflora

Ipheion uniflorum

Iris

Iris

Iris family.
True bulb or rhizome; most are deciduous.
Blooms at various times between late winter and summer.

Location: Variously adapted to meadow, woodland, rock garden, border, miniature garden, raised bed, alpine house, container.

Soil: Well-drained, neutral to alkaline soils.

Care: Feed and water moderately and decrease or discontinue after the bloom season.

Exposure: Sun, with few exceptions.

From a diverse range of Northern Hemisphere habitats comes one of the most spectacular and deservedly popular groups of bulbs. The flowers of all the irises have a distinctive three-part symmetry, but in other respects flowers and plants vary. In this book the irises are discussed in two major groups: rhizomatous irises and bulbous irises. Each group contains various subgroups and species.

Rhizomatous Irises. The majority of cultivated iris species and hybrids grow from rhizomes. They fall into three categories: crested, beardless, and bearded. All should be planted just at the surface of the soil, not buried.

Bearded Iris Hybrids. The vast majority of garden irises are the late-spring and early-summer blooming (and sometimes reblooming) bearded iris hybrids.

They are sold by virtually every general nursery and bulb supplier. Flowers range in color over the entire spectrum, including striking bicolors and even browns and near-blacks; only true red is missing. All are excellent for cutting. Most thrive in beds and perennial borders—the smaller ones in rock gardens—wherever there is some frost, but the winter temperature remains above –30° F. All accept most soils—if drainage is good—and periods of dryness.

In early spring, fertilize lightly with a complete fertilizer and lime, in equal parts. Overwatering and overfertilizing are harmful. Except in the hottest western climates, give them full sun. Plant or transplant the rhizomes 1 to 2½ feet apart, from midsummer to early fall. Plant them horizontally, not quite buried. Every four or five years, dig and divide them, cutting away old, leafless, woody portions of the rhizomes and letting the cuts dry for several hours before replanting.

Watch for evidence of iris borers: In the spring, look for bleeding of leaves where borers have entered. Remove affected parts, including portions of the rhizomes that borers have entered through the leaves.

The American Iris Society has created an elaborate classification system for bearded iris hybrids, based on plant height, from Miniature Dwarf Iris (to 8 inches) to Tall Bearded Iris (27 to 48 inches). Unless a bulb catalog designates another class for a hybrid, you can assume that it is a Tall Bearded Iris.

Beardless Irises. Beardless irises (misleadingly named because several other groups are also beardless) include a number of European, American, and Asian species. All are available from specialists, and some from general nurseries.

From the West Coast of the United States come spring- and early-summer-blooming *I. douglasiana* (Douglas iris), *I. innominata*, and other less-available species, along with the popular Pacific Coast hybrids. All are ideally suited to the moderate climates of the Pacific Northwest and coastal California; most are hardy to 10° F. Handsomely veined and blotched flowers on 12- to 20-inch stems range from white to gray, bronze, gold, mauve, blue, pink, and cream. Some are strikingly bicolored. All are excellent cut flowers. They thrive where summers are moderate, in sun or light shade. *I. douglasiana* is less amenable than many others to summer watering.

Iris reticulata

Far better adapted to summer watering, even to marshy soils, are other beardless irises: *I. kaempferi* (Japanese iris) and its hybrids, notably the Higo strain; and Louisiana irises, hybrids of several southern and midwestern species. Both irises are large and showy. *I. kaempferi* bears 6- to 9-inch, flattened crepelike flowers, on 2-foot stems in June. Louisiana irises, to 4 feet tall, bear 4- to 5-inch flowers in nearly every color in late spring. Both need acid soil; for *I. kaempferi* soil should be only moist, not wet, after the annual period of growth ends.

The Spuria irises, including several named varieties in a wide range of intense colors, grow to 2 feet or taller and bloom in late spring and early summer. They require rich, moist, neutral soil and are hardy to –30° F. Plant them in the fall.

The many varieties of *I. sibirica* (Siberian iris) are excellent for garden borders and cutting. Suited to acid to neutral garden soils in sunny or lightly shaded gardens, they are hardy to –30° F and do best where there is some winter frost. In June Siberian iris produces handsome, often ruffled blue, white, purple, or red flowers, several to a 2- to 3-foot stem. Grown in deep, rich, moist soil, it forms dense clumps that remain green long after flowering and seldom require dividing. Plant in the fall, and divide in the spring or fall.

I. foetidissima (scarlet-seeded iris), 2 feet tall, evergreen with curiously colored, inconspicuous spring flowers, provides split pods of startling scarlet or orange seeds for the autumn garden or dried flower arrangements. This adaptable iris grows in sun or shade, in good or poor soil where temperatures remain above 0° F. Plant in the spring or fall.

Bearded Irises. Bearded (Pogon) irises, so named because of the pattern of hairs on the basal portion of the falls, or outer petals, include most cultivated irises. A little-grown, challenging group considered by many iris experts to be the most beautiful and choice of irises is the Aril group, including an especially attractive subgroup, Oncocyclus irises, some of which are becoming available from specialists. Spring-flowering *I. susiana*, from Asia Minor, has spectacular large, purplish flowers whose coloration is created by fine patterns of blackish purple veins and dots on a gray field. *I. sari* has brownish purple veins on a yellow field. Grow them and other available Oncocyclus species and hybrids, including the Arilbreds, exactly as you would grow Juno irises, described under "Bulbous Irises" below. Add some garden lime or dolomite limestone to the soil to supply needed calcium and magnesium.

Crested Irises. Crested irises, so named because of the small crest at the base of each outer petal, include several Asian and North American species available commercially from specialists and occasionally from general nurseries.

I. cristata (dwarf crested iris), a 6-inch-tall native of the eastern United States woodlands, produces lavender-blue or white flowers with deep yellow crests, in late spring or early summer. Its thin rhizomes should be planted during the fall in acid, moist, well-drained soil, in a partially shaded woodland or rock garden area. It is hardy to –30° F, and where it's well adapted, it will colonize. Propagate it by division in late summer.

I. japonica, from Japan and China, bears frilly, yellow-crested, yellow-and-white-spotted lilac flowers on branching 18-inch stems in late spring. Hardy only to 10° F, it is an excellent container plant for the greenhouse. Plant in acid, well-drained soil, in sun or light shade.

The similar *I. tectorum* (roof iris), from China, bears 6-inch lilac, white, or lavender blue flowers on 12- to 18-inch stems in late spring. This evergreen is suited to gardens of humid-climate areas that do not get colder than –20° F, where it accepts most well-drained soils, dryness, and sun or partial shade, and often naturalizes in rich, well-mulched soils. Plant rhizomes in the spring or fall, and propagate in the spring or fall by division.

Bulbous Irises. Described below are three groups of irises whose underground parts are true bulbs.

Iris innominata

Iris kaempferi 'Pink Pearl'

Reticulata Irises. From Asia Minor comes the Reticulata group of dwarf beardless irises, with netted tunics around the bulbs and yellow, blue, lavender, violet-purple, or multicolored flowers, many with intricate contrasting markings. They are 3 to 8 inches high, with flowers from 2 to 3 inches wide. They bloom in late winter or very early spring. The foliage reaches maturity after flowering has ended. *I. reticulata* (violet-purple and blue with yellow markings), *I. danfordiae* (yellow), *I. bakerana* (violet with yellow markings), *I. winogradowii* (yellow with orange markings), and other species and many named hybrids are widely sold. They are suited to sunny rock gardens, alpine houses, frames, and raised beds, and they force easily (plant 9 to 12 in a 4-inch pot). Planted 6 or 8 inches deep and mulched in the coldest areas, they thrive in areas that get some frost, but no colder than –30° F. If planted in pots, they should be repotted every year. Most like nearly neutral soil, though *I. danfordiae* prefers slight acidity. All require regular feeding and watering until the foliage dies back; then they prefer dryness and heat. Reticulatas can be propagated by offsets or divisions in late summer or early fall.

Iris winogradowii

Iris sari

Xiphion Irises. Familiar as excellent cut flowers are the larger-scale, mid- to late-spring-flowering Dutch irises. These hybrids of *I. xiphium* (Spanish iris) come from southern Europe and Morocco and have yellow, gold, blue, purple, violet, bronze, white, or bi-colored 4-inch flowers, borne on 15- to 25-inch stems. All are members of the Xiphion group. All thrive in sunny beds and containers, and are hardy to –10° F. In colder climates they can be mulched, or lifted and stored during dormancy, like gladiolus. (See page 65.) Dutch iris, however, prefers a soil temperature of 60° F at planting time. Plant bulbs of all these types 3 to 5 inches deep and 5 inches apart in the fall, or 1 inch deep, four or five to a 6-inch pot. Water during active growth; reduce or stop watering after foliage withers.

Juno Irises. Juno irises are available only from specialists. These natives of Asia Minor have a leafy central stem from whose leaf axils small flowers grow in spring. Occasionally available are 18-inch-tall *I. bucharica* (Bokhara iris), with yellow-and-white blossoms, and *I. magnifica*, to 2 feet tall, bearing soft lilac flowers with white crests and yellow-blotched outer petals. In the fall Junos should be planted 4 inches deep in rich, fast-draining soil mulched with gravel, in hot sun. Overhead watering is harmful to Junos. Fertilize in the spring with a complete fertilizer. After blooming, fertilize with a high-phosphorus fertilizer and lime, then keep them completely dry until the next growing season. A bulb frame or an alpine house is necessary in most climate areas.

Ismene

See *Hymenocallis*, page 71.

Ixia

Corn lily

Iris family.
Corm; deciduous.
Blooms spring or early summer.

Location: Rock garden, alpine house, container, border.

Soil: Well drained, sandy, neutral to alkaline.

Care: Water after weather cools in autumn, throughout winter and spring; then dry out, or dig and store, until cool fall weather. No fertilizing is necessary in good garden soil.

Exposure: Sun.

Ixia, an ancient Greek name denoting a plant with variable coloration, perfectly suits this producer of many-hued flowers. Its common name refers to the corn fields that it prefers in its South African habitat. Unlike its similar cousins hesperantha and geissorhiza, it has been grown widely for nearly 200 years, and many ixia hybrids have been developed. It is hardy to –10° F. Flowers are borne on wiry stems 10 to 36 inches tall, above narrow-bladed leaves. Ixia makes a handsome pot plant, and it lends color and grassy texture to a border. It is a durable cut flower; the stems last up to two weeks, but the flowers open wide only in bright light. Yellow and white blossoms are fragrant.

Plant corms in the fall, 4 to 5 inches deep and 3 to 4 inches apart in the garden or 1 inch deep in pots, five or six per 6-inch pot. Because the flowers close in even light shade, grow them in full sun. Stake as necessary. If you dig and store the corms, store them without packing material. If you leave ixia in the garden over winter, mulch it well for protection from cold. It is easy to propagate from cormlets in the fall, or seeds in the spring.

I. maculata grows to 2 feet tall and bears golden yellow to orange flowers with purplish black centers, often with a small orange or yellow star in the middle.

I. paniculata may grow up to 3 feet tall but is usually shorter. It has creamy white flowers, often with purplish black centers.

I. viridiflora grows to 18 inches tall and has startling greenish blue flowers with purplish black centers.

A multitude of ixia hybrids are sold in a wide range of colors.

Ixia hybrid

Ixiolirion tataricum

Ixia hybrid

Ixiolirion tataricum

Ixiolirion tataricum

(I. montanum, I. pallasii)
Siberian lily, Tartar lily

Amaryllis family.
True bulb; deciduous.
Blooms in late spring.

Location: Border, container.

Soil: Most fast-draining garden soils.

Care: Water regularly and feed lightly with a complete fertilizer during period of growth.

Exposure: Sun.

Starlike, 1½-inch blue blossoms, up to 18 per stem, make *Ixiolirion tataricum* a showy garden flower. Blossoms are borne on slender 16-inch stems among grasslike leaves, and are equally attractive in the garden or in a vase. This native of Asia is occasionally sold by specialists.

Plant bulbs 3 inches deep and 3 inches apart, in the fall. They are hardy to –10° F, but mulch them if you get heavy frosts. You can grow tartar lilies in colder areas if you dig and store the bulbs over winter, then plant them in spring. Propagate by offsets in the fall.

Lachenalia aloides

Lapeirousia jacquinii

Lachenalia

Cape cowslip

Lily family.
True bulb; deciduous.
Blooms late winter or early spring.

Location: Alpine house, container, border, rock garden, greenhouse, house.

Soil: Fast draining, sandy, acid to neutral.

Care: Water moderately through growth and blooming period, until leaves start to yellow; dry off over summer in ground or pots, or dig and store cool in dry packing medium until cool, rainy fall weather. Provide periodic light feeding during growing period.

Exposure: Sun or partial shade.

Nodding, waxy flowers on spotted, fleshy stems above pairs of beautiful spotted and pebble-textured leaves make this large group of South African bulbs especially important to bulb fanciers. Many species are extravagantly variegated with, for example, green, purple, red, and yellow mixed in the same blossoms; others are white or another solid color. The blossoms are long-lasting on the plants and in vases. Lachenalia species are beginning to be sold by some specialists. Many new varieties are being developed in South Africa and should soon be available here.

Plant bulbs in the fall, up to 1 inch deep and 2 inches apart, in large clumps of a single species, or up to three or four bulbs per 6-inch pot or bulb pan.

L. aloides (L. tricolor), widely sold, grows 6 to 12 inches tall, often has spotted leaves, and bears tubular yellow flowers with red-tipped green inner segments as well as red or reddish buds and stem tips. Other color forms include 'Aurea' (bright orange-yellow), 'Conspicua' (orange with purple margins and yellow-red tips), 'Luteola' (green-tipped lemon yellow), 'Nelsonii' (bright yellow with green tinge), and 'Quadricolor' (red, greenish yellow, green, and reddish purple).

L. bulbiferum (L. pendula) grows from 6 to 12 inches tall and has long, drooping tubular flowers, coral red with green and purple tips.

L. mutabilis grows to 1 foot tall and bears a delicately tapered spike of sky-blue buds above iridescent bluish mauve flowers whose inner parts are yellow, aging to crimson. The flowers look best if lightly shaded.

L. orchioides has a pair of spreading, sometimes spotted leaves and a 9- to 14-inch spike bearing fragrant pale yellow, pink, white, or blue-green iridescent flowers with mauve-tinged creamy inner parts.

L. unicolor bears a 5-inch spike densely covered with violet-colored flowers.

L. viridiflora bears tubular turquoise flowers with a lacquerlike sheen. It blooms around Christmas.

Lachenalia
tricolor

Lapeirousia
fabricii

Lapeirousia

Iris family.
Corm; deciduous.
Blooms variably, depending on species.

Location: Rock garden, border, container, alpine house, greenhouse.

Soil: Fast draining, sandy, acid to neutral.

Care: Water regularly during growth and blooming; dry off during dormancy, and except where acclimated, store warm in pots or dry packing material.

Exposure: Sun or, especially in hot climates, partial shade.

Lapeirousia, which formerly included species now classified by botanists as Anomatheca (see page 41), is a group of African plants that bear bright flowers in the summer or in late winter or early spring, depending on species. Most lapeirousias are tender and some require seasonal dryness, so in most climate areas they are best grown in pots for protection.

Plant corms 4 inches deep and 4 to 6 inches apart in the garden, or 1 inch deep and six or seven per 6-inch pot or bulb pan. Plant summer-growing species in spring, and winter-growing species in fall. Propagate from offsets.

A summer grower, L. erythrantha (L. sandersonii) grows to 12 to 18 inches and bears branched stems of showy whitish, lilac-blue, or deep reddish mauve flowers with dark marks on the bases of lower petals.

These are two winter growers:
L. fabricii grows up to 6 inches or taller and bears white to pale red flowers with dark red stripes and red-spotted bases of lower petals.

L. jacquinii, similar in habit to L. fabricii, bears 1-inch blue flowers.

Leucojum

Snowflake

Amaryllis family.
True bulb; deciduous.
Bloom season varies with species.

Location: Mixed border, meadow, woodland, rock garden, alpine house, container, seasonally indoors.

Soil: Nearly any well-drained garden soil will do, though sandy, organic loam is best.

Care: Water regularly and feed occasionally with complete fertilizer except during dormancy, when soil must not be allowed to dry completely.

Exposure: Sun or partial shade.

Lush foliage and small nodding white bells from ¾ to 1½ inches wide, with petal tips spotted bright green, make this hardy garden favorite easy to spot. All species should be planted, transplanted, or divided after foliage has withered. All look best if planted in large clumps or bold drifts, bulbs 4 to 5 inches deep and 4 to 6 inches apart, and left undivided for many years.

All species make excellent cut flowers, lasting up to a week.

L. aestivum (giant or summer snowflake) is a mid- to late-spring-blooming native of the damp stream banks of Europe and Asia Minor. Its 1-foot stems bear two to eight bells. 'Gravetye Giant' has large flowers (to 1½ inches wide) on stems to 18 inches tall. This widely available species is hardy to –20° F, and adapts readily to heavy, moist soils.

L. autumnale (autumn snowflake), from southern Europe and North Africa, prefers sandy soil, fast drainage, and full sun. Its 2- to 9-inch slender stems bear one to four white flowers lightly tinged with pink, from late summer to midfall. This widely available species adapts well where temperatures do not drop below –10° F.

L. vernum (spring snowflake), from Central Europe, produces one or two fragrant flowers per stem, among 9-inch leaves, in late winter or early spring. This species adapts to many growing conditions but prefers moist soil. It is amenable to container culture in a frame or cool alpine house. Spring snowflake is hardy to –20° F, and does best where it gets some winter frost. The bulb sold as *L. vernum* is often *L. aestivum*.

Leucojum aestivum

Leucojum aestivum

Lilium speciosum

Lilium

Lily

Lily family.
True bulb; deciduous.
Blooms midspring to early fall, depending on type.

Location: Border, rock garden, woodland, meadow, container, greenhouse, house.

Soil: Deep, well drained, organic, acid to neutral.

Care: Water regularly during period of growth and blooming; reduce watering, but never dry out during dormancy. Feed lightly with a low-nitrogen, high-potassium fertilizer when annual growth begins.

Exposure: Sun or light shade, especially in hot areas; shade on ground above bulbs.

Some blaze with color, others are sedate; some dominate their garden places, others are modest in scale; some scent the garden, others appeal only to the eye—but every lily is magnificent. Throughout recorded history this native of the Northern Hemisphere has stood apart as one of the special garden and container plants and cut flowers. One species has even gained the status of a religious emblem. Modern hybridization has increased the variety, colors, and forms of lilies and made them even more adaptable, vigorous, disease resistant, and easy to grow. It is principally the modern hybrids that are sold and grown today, though a number of splendid species, some of which are described below, are available and deserve wider cultivation.

With few exceptions, lilies are hardy (usually to –40° F) and grow well in most of the country, though they do not favor dry heat. Because the bulbs have no outer covering and store no food, they must be protected and nourished by cool, moist, rich soil. Planted in beds, drifts, or clumps, they are a focus of beauty in the garden. You can plant in either spring or fall, during dormancy (except for Madonna lily, which should be planted in late summer).

Buy fresh bulbs that are properly packed, with roots and scales firm and undamaged. Planting depth is determined mainly by the size of the bulb: the rule of thumb is to plant at a depth three times the vertical diameter of the bulb, so that a 2-inch-high bulb has 6 inches of soil above it. (Again, Madonna lily is an exception and is planted only an inch or two deep.) It is very important that lilies that produce stem roots above the bulbs be planted sufficiently deep.

Space larger lilies at least 1 foot apart. Mulch around the plants after growth begins. Leave lilies in the garden undisturbed until clumps are so crowded that they begin to decline in vigor. Stake top-heavy lilies in windy sites. Mulch heavily in the fall as protection against alternate thawing and freezing.

Propagate by bulblets, which form on most lilies' underground stems, or by removing scales and placing them in a sealed bag of moist peat moss or other medium at around 70° F, or by planting bulbils. See page 31.

Many lilies can be forced indoors; see page 19. For container culture, use a large pot and plant three or four bulbs deep enough for stem roots to form if you are planting a stem-rooting type, and leave room to add soil as the plants grow. After blooming, gradually dry off the bulbs and store in cool, moist packing material.

Lilies are susceptible to several viruses, particularly lily mosaic, usually transmitted by aphids (which are themselves a threat). Do not propagate lilies with virus diseases; all parts of an infected plant have the virus, except for the seed.

Most lilies are superb cut flowers, lasting up to eight days. When you cut them, be careful to leave on the plant as much stem and foliage as possible, to enable the bulbs to flower the following year.

Mid-Century hybrid lilies

Lilium longiflorum

The Royal Horticultural Society in England and the North American Lily Society have developed a standard classification system for lilies. Lilies in the divisions listed below are widely sold.

Division 1: Asiatic Hybrids. These hybrids are early flowering, 2 to 5 feet high with 4- to 6-inch flowers in reds, pinks, oranges, yellows, lavender, and white. Growth is compact. Subdivisions are Upright-Flowering, Outward-Facing and Pendant-Flowering. Flowers are borne singly or in umbels. This division includes the Mid-Century hybrids which were developed for easy cultivation. Asiatic hybrids root above the bulbs (they are stem rooting).

Division 2: Martagon Hybrids. These hybrids blossom in late spring; they are 3 to 6 feet high, with 3- to 4-inch flowers in white, yellow, lavender, orange, brown, lilac, tangerine, and mahogany. This division includes the Paisley hybrids. Like the Asiatic hybrids, they are stemrooting.

Division 3: Candidum Hybrids. These hybrids bloom in spring and early summer; they grow 3 to 4 feet in height and have 4- to 5-inch flowers. The division includes hybrids resulting from crosses between L. candidum and L. chalcedonicum. Plant bulbs in late summer, only 1 or 2 inches deep.

Division 4: American Hybrids. These are late spring and early summer flowering, 4 to 8 feet in height, with 4- to 6-inch flowers. They are hybrids of North American native lilies, including the Bellingham hybrids and San Gabriel strain.

Division 5: Longiflorum Hybrids. The familiar white Easter lily or white trumpet lily, L. longiflorum, and its hybrids are forced for sale at Easter, and bloom in midsummer in the garden.

Division 6: Trumpet Hybrids. These are summer-flowering lilies that grow 4 to 6 feet tall with 6- to 10-inch flowers. This division includes the Aurelian and Olympic hybrids, which have trumpet-shaped blossoms. Some other members of this division have starlike, pendant, or flat, open flowers.

Division 7: Oriental Hybrids. These hybrids bloom in late summer; they grow 2 to 8 feet high, with flowers to 12 inches. These are bowl-shaped, flat-faced flowers with recurving petals. They are available in white, deep reds, pinks, and bicolors.

Division 8: Species Lilies. This division includes long-grown species native to North America, Europe, and Asia. The following are some of the best for gardens, though many other suitable species are sold.

L. auratum (gold-banded lily) grows 3 to 8 feet tall and bears up to 35 fragrant flowers per stem. Each outward-facing flower is bowl shaped and up to 1 foot wide. The color varies, but the most typical is white spotted with crimson, each petal with a central yellow stripe. It blooms in late summer or early fall. Shallow planting is best. Native to Japan, L. auratum thrives in cool seaside climates. The variety platyphyllum has broader, more numerous leaves and especially large flowers with fewer spots.

L. candidum (Madonna lily) is native to grassy slopes of Asia Minor. See **Division 3.** It has large, fragrant, trumpet flowers on 2- to 6-foot stems and requires shallow planting in a neutral to alkaline soil.

L. columbianum (Columbia lily), from the mountains of Oregon and British Columbia, bears 20 to 40 golden-orange, purple-dotted flowers on 2- to 5-foot stems. It likes woodland conditions.

L. kelloggii, from northwestern California, grows from 3 to 4 feet tall and bears up to 20 nodding, fragrant, cream to pink flowers that age to mauve. Grow it in mild woodland conditions.

L. martagon (Turk's-cap lily), from a broad area of Europe and Asia, is very hardy. On 3- to 6-foot stems it bears a dozen to 30 or more flowers whose petals bend back sharply. Pinkish purple to claret red flowers are purple-dotted toward their centers.

L. pardalinum (Leopard lily), native to California and Oregon, bears 1 to 24 or more fragrant flowers 4 to 4 inches wide, orange-red with crimson-tipped petals recurved like those of L. martagon and spotted with maroon. The pollen is orange. Stems are 4 to 8 feet tall. It is a prolific producer of bulbets. L. pardalinum 'Giganteum', which is vigorous and easy to grow, is often available.

L. regale (Regal lily), a garden favorite native to Tibet, bears umbels of fragrant trumpet flowers, white with yellow centers and purple or lilac undersides, atop 4- to 6-foot stems. Variety 'Album' has pure white flowers.

Lycoris

Amaryllis family.
True bulb; deciduous.
Blooms in late summer or fall.

Location: Border, container, alpine house.

Soil: Fast draining, sandy, organic, acid to neutral.

Care: Water regularly and feed with balanced fertilizer during growing period, fall to spring; dry off during summer dormancy. Some summer rain is tolerated if soil drains rapidly.

Exposure: Sun.

Appearing almost as suddenly as mushrooms, the leafless stems of lycoris emerge from the ground to lend much-needed color to the late-season garden. The leaves emerge later and last until late spring. *L. radiata* and closely allied species are almost indistinguishable from the closely related nerine, and *L. squamigera* resembles another close relation, *Amaryllis belladonna*. Flowers of all lycoris radiate from the top of each stem, and the filaments arch outward beyond the petals—very noticeably in *L. radiata*—to create an elegant, spidery effect. All are superb cut flowers. The species listed below are widely sold by general suppliers and specialists.

In early August, before flower stems appear, plant *L. radiata* bulbs 3 to 4 inches deep, *L. squamigera* bulbs 5 to 6 inches deep, and both 6 inches apart. In containers plant bulbs with the necks exposed, one bulb per 6-inch pot. Wait several years to repot. Propagate by offsets in early August.

L. africana (*L. aurea, Amaryllis aurea*), native from China to Burma, is popularly called hurricane lily and golden spider lily. Its stems are 18 inches tall, and the flowers are yellow with recurved petals with wavy edges. It is hardy to –10° F.

L. radiata (*Amaryllis radiata*), spider lily, from China and Japan, is quite similar to closely allied *L. africana* except in color.

L. squamigera (*Amaryllis hallii*), from Japan, called magic lily and resurrection lily, bears large, smooth-petaled, rose-pink flowers with an amethyst fringe on stems 1½ to 2 feet tall. It blooms best if the bulbs are chilled during the winter.

Lycoris radiata

Milla biflora

Mexican star

Allium family.
True bulb; deciduous.
Blooms intermittently spring to fall outdoors, winter and spring indoors.

Location: Border, rock garden, container, house, greenhouse.

Soil: Well drained, neutral to alkaline.

Care: Water generously and provide occasional light feeding. Dry off after flowering, and store in container, or in ground if above –10° F.

Exposure: Sun or very light shade.

From the American Southwest and Mexico comes Mexican star, a grassy plant with 12- to 18-inch erect flower stalks bearing umbels of one to six fragrant white 2-inch blossoms. Each petal of the starlike flower has a green nerve down the middle. Where it stays warmer than –10° F, the plant can remain outside all year. Container culture or winter storage is necessary elsewhere. Plant corms 3 to 4 inches deep and 3 to 4 inches apart in the garden, or 1½ inches deep in pots, five or six bulbs per 5-inch pot. Soil mix should contain some ground limestone. It grows best where night temperatures during the growing season remain about 60° F. Propagate in fall from offsets.

Milla biflora is sometimes sold wrongly as *Bessera elegans*.

Plants sold as *Milla uniflora* are *Ipheion uniflorum*. See page 72.

Lycoris radiata

Milla biflora

Milla biflora

Montebretia

See *Crocosmia × crocosmiiflora*, page 52, and *Tritonia*, page 90.

Moraea

Butterfly iris

Iris family.
Corm; deciduous (winter and some summer growers) or evergreen (other summer growers).
Blooms in winter or spring, or in summer, depending on species.

Location: Border, rock garden, greenhouse, alpine house, container.

Soil: Well drained, sandy, organic, acid to neutral.

Care: Water during period of growth and blooming; dry off during dormancy. In good garden soils no feeding is necessary.

Exposure: Sun.

For information about plants usually sold as *M. iridioides* and *M. bicolor*, see *Dietes*, page 58.

Moraeas, resplendent South African flowers unsurpassed for elegant form, need make no apologies to their Northern Hemisphere relatives, the irises. In scale they range from dwarfs, 2 to 6 inches tall, to imposing plants 3 feet tall. The flowers are white or shades of buff, red, pink, purple, brown, yellow, orange, blue, and mauve. Many have contrasting circular or triangular markings that function as nectar guides for pollinating insects. Each flower lasts a short time, but moraeas tend to bloom profusely over many weeks.

Species that grow and bloom in the summer require summer watering, and with good drainage they tolerate water during dormancy. Winter growers bloom in the winter or the spring and require drying off in the summer. Plant dormant moraea corms in fall or spring, in cool weather, with smaller species 1 to 2 inches deep, larger species 3 to 4 inches deep. Plant five or six corms in a 6-inch bulb pan. In areas that get summer rainfall, dry off, dig, and store the winter growers over summer. Except in frost-free areas, dry off, dig, and store the deciduous summer growers over winter at a cool temperature. Propagate by offsets during dormancy, or by seeds. Plant the seeds of summer growers in the spring and the seeds of winter growers in the fall. The seeds of winter growers germinate when the temperature is in the 40s.

The following are some winter-growing species:

M. aristata (M. glaucopis, M. tricuspidata), one of the peacock moraeas (so called because the brilliant nectar guides at the bases of petals suggest the "eyes" of peacock feathers), has white flowers with bright blue blotches outlined in black.

M. ciliata, a 4-inch-tall miniature, has 1½-inch white flowers flushed with pale blue; the undersides of the petals are pale bronze. The flowers are scented.

M. gigandra grows 2 feet tall and has 3-inch, lilac to deep purple flowers with a flash of cobalt blue above a black center.

M. neopavonia (peacock iris), one of the peacock moraeas like M. aristata, grows 1 to 2½ feet tall and has 2-inch, variably colored flowers, usually brilliant orange or yellow with navy blue or black nectar guides.

M. papilionacea, a 4- or 5-inch-tall miniature, has salmon or orange flowers; most forms have yellow nectar guides.

M. tricolor, another miniature, varies in color. The bright red form is especially prized by collectors. Flowers are clove scented.

M. villosa, a peacock moraea, grows to 2 feet tall and has 2-inch cream, pink, lilac, or purple flowers with large blue or greenish nectar guides, which are often encircled by a contrasting color.

Here are three summer growers that you may be able to find.

M. huttonii grows to 4 feet tall with evergreen leaves 4 feet long or longer and bears yellow flowers with dark yellow nectar guides outlined in brownish purple.

M. natalensis grows to 15 inches tall and bears lilac flowers with yellow nectar guides edged with mauve.

Moraea neopavonia

Moraea villosa

Muscari armeniacum

Muscari

Grape hyacinth

Lily family
True bulb; deciduous.
Blooms in spring.

Location: Woodland, border, rock garden, meadow, container.

Soil: Well drained, sandy, acid to neutral, not too rich.

Care: Requires little summer watering; water moderately in other seasons. Little feeding is necessary.

Exposure: Sun or light shade.

Dense spikes of urn-shaped flowers ("grapes") that are most often blue, wide adaptation and ease of cultivation, and a tendency to naturalize quickly make grape hyacinths popular in gardens everywhere. This group of bulbs from the Mediterranean area and adjacent regions looks at home in short grass, woodland edges, borders, and rock gardens. It is attractive with primroses, miniature daffodils, candytuft, and other small-scale spring garden flowers. Many muscari are lightly fragrant, and all are useful as cut flowers, lasting up to 7 days. They can be forced (see page 19).

In the fall plant bulbs in the garden, 5 inches deep and 1 to 4 inches apart, depending on size or species, or in pots, 1 inch deep and 10 to 12 per 6-inch pot. Dry off pot-grown muscari after blooming. Propagation is quite easy from offsets, division of clumps, and sowing of seeds.

Muscari armeniacum

The following species are moderately to widely available:

M. armeniacum grows to 9 inches tall and has blue flowers with a fine white fringe. Established bulbs produce leaves in the fall. 'Blue Spike' has double, soft blue flowers; 'Saphir' has deep blue, white-fringed flowers that are especially long lasting in the garden or a vase; 'Early Giant' is cobalt-blue with white fringe.

M. azureum (Hyacinthus azureus, Hyacinthella azurea) grows to 8 inches tall, has bright blue tubular flowers on large, dense spikes, and blooms very early. White and light blue forms are sold.

M. botryoides (common grape hyacinth) grows to 1 foot tall and has dense spikes of white flowers. A form with white-rimmed navy blue flowers is sold, and occasionally a pale rose one. M. botryoides can be forced.

M. comosum (tassel hyacinth) grows to 12 inches tall and has greenish spikes with purplish tips. 'Plumosum' and 'Monstrosum', both called feather hyacinth, have shredded flowers, the former, blue violet; the latter, reddish purple.

M. latifolium grows to 1 foot tall and bears dense spikes of flowers, the lower ones deep indigo and the upper ones pale blue violet.

M. racemosum (M. moschatum) grows to 10 inches tall and bears heavily scented purple flowers that turn yellow as they age.

M. tubergenianum grows to 1 foot high and bears dense spikes with a lower portion of deep blue, and an upper portion of bright blue.

Triandrus daffodil 'Thalia'

Narcissus

Daffodil, Narcissus, and Jonquil

Amaryllis family.
True bulb; deciduous.
Blooms late winter or spring.

Location: Border, woodland, meadow, rock garden, container, house, alpine house.

Soil: Sandy, organic garden soil produces lush plants and is desirable for most of the hybrids, but any well-drained soil will do.

Care: Water regularly through the growing season from autumn until foliage begins to die. A light fertilizing makes for vigor in hybrids: before planting, thoroughly mix a small amount of bone meal or superphosphate into the soil.

Exposure: Sun or light shade.

Easy to grow and naturalize—and richly perfumed, besides—daffodils have for centuries been among the most popular garden plants. Ancestors of garden daffodils come from Europe and Asia; the greatest concentration of species is around the Mediterranean. They are commonly (and properly) referred to collectively as daffodils, though some people call them all jonquils. However, the term jonquils properly be-

Narcissus 'King Alfred'

longs only to *N. jonquilla* and a few other closely allied daffodils. The whole genus of daffodils is *Narcissus* (their Latin name), but a small group of intensely fragrant daffodils also bears the common name of narcissus. By whatever name, daffodils are incomparable, with their trumpeted or cupped, sometimes double, flowers of yellow, white, gold, orange, pink, reddish, or bicolors. All are excellent cut flowers, lasting four to six days.

With exceptions, such as *N. tazetta*, daffodils are adapted to most climates of the country. Plant bulbs of large species 8 inches deep, and smaller ones 5 inches deep, in early fall in the North, and southward progressively later, to November or December. Space bulbs 2 to 6 inches apart, depending on the size of the species or variety. For container culture, including forcing (see page 19), plant three large doubled-nosed bulbs (or more small ones) per 6-inch bulb pan or pot.

Position daffodils where their collapsing, yellowing foliage will not be unsightly; don't remove the leaves before they have yellowed completely, or the bulbs might fail to bloom the next spring. When clumps are so dense that they decline in vigor, dig and divide them in late summer, as soon as the foliage has died. Propagate at the same time by offsets, but don't separate an offset until it has developed a basal plate (the flat bottom from which roots grow). The toxic bulbs are avoided by deer and rodents, but snails and slugs are undeterred. Other potential but infrequent problems are virus (see page 31), and basal rot in warm climates (see page 32).

The following 12 divisions of *Narcissus* are recognized by the American Daffodil Society. This system or modifications of it are used in many commercial catalogs. All but the tenth division refer to hybrids of garden origin. Many varieties, hundreds in some cases, belong to these groups. Various daffodils, including many of the species, are widely available.

Division 1: Trumpet Daffodils. One flower per stem; trumpet as long as or longer than the petals.

Division 2: Long-Cupped Daffodils. One flower per stem; cup more than one third but less than full length of the petals.

Division 3: Short-Cupped Daffodils. One flower per stem; cup (shallow trumpet) not more than one third the length of the petals.

Division 4: Double Daffodils. Double flowers.

Division 5: Triandrus Daffodils. Characteristics of *N. triandrus* predominant; see below.

Division 6: Cyclamineus Daffodils. Characteristics of *N. cyclamineus* predominant; see below.

Division 7: Jonquilla Daffodils. Characteristics of the *N. jonquilla* group predominant; see below.

Division 8: Tazetta Daffodils. Characteristics of *N. tazetta* group predominant; see below.

Division 9: Poeticus Daffodils. Characteristics of *N. poeticus* predominant; see below.

Division 10: Species and Wild Forms and Wild Hybrids. A number are listed and described below.

Division 11: Split-Corona Daffodils. Cups irregularly split for at least one third of their length; in many varieties spread wide enough to cover or nearly cover petals.

Division 12: Miscellaneous Daffodils. Any not fitting into other divisions.

Listed here are a number of wild daffodils (Division 10), including those used to create the hybrids of Divisions 5 through 9.

N. bulbocodium (petticoat daffodil) has rushlike leaves to 15 inches tall, tiny petals, and a 1-inch flaring "petticoat" trumpet. Several varieties differ in flower size and in color—bright yellow to nearly white.

N. cyclamineus grows to 1 foot tall and has solitary, nodding, deep yellow flowers with a short, wavy-edged cup and petals that bend backward.

N. × odorus (Campernelle jonquil), about 1 foot high, bears two to four bright yellow, very fragrant, 2½-inch flowers. A double form is sometimes sold.

N. jonquilla (jonquil) grows to 18 inches tall and bears two to six fragrant golden-yellow flowers per stem. A double form is occasionally sold.

N. tazetta includes paperwhite narcissus and Chinese sacred lily, which are all popularly termed *narcissus*. Clusters of powerfully fragrant flowers grow atop stems to 18 inches tall. There are pure white, pure yellow, white and yellow, and yellow and gold varieties.

N. triandrus (angel's tears) on 1-foot stems bears pure white to pale yellow flowers, solitary or in clusters of up to six, with cups ¾-inch deep and bent-back petals. Leaves are rushlike.

Narcissus bulbocodium

Nerine

Amaryllis family.
True bulb; deciduous.
Blooms in fall.

Location: Container, alpine house, greenhouse, border.

Soil: Fast draining, sandy, acid to neutral.

Care: Water and provide regular, light feeding through winter and spring; except for N. bowdenii, which is a summer grower and requires gradual drying off in early summer and complete dryness from mid-summer to flowering.

Exposure: Sun or light shade.

Strikingly similar to its cousin Lycoris radiata in appearance and culture, nerine is even less hardy (except for N. bowdenii), and is nearly always grown in containers. All species are from South Africa, and most are difficult to locate.

Plant bulbs from late summer to late fall. Use one bulb per 4-inch pot, two or three in a larger pot, with the tops of the bulbs above soil level. Don't water a newly planted bulb; wait for the flower stalk to appear. Leave bulbs in pots or garden beds until they are crowded. Propagate from offsets at planting time.

N. bowdenii grows to 15 inches tall with pale pink to rose pink flowers marked in deeper tones. It adapts well where the temperature doesn't drop below 20° F. It is widely sold.

N. flexuosa has pale pink flowers with crisped petal edges. Grows up to 3 feet.

N. sarniensis (Guernsey lily) grows to 18 inches tall and has flowers of crimson overlaid by iridescent gold and prominent bright red stamens. There are bright red and salmon red forms.

Nerine
bowdenii

Ornithogalum
narbonense

Nerine bowdenii

Ornithogalum

Lily family.
True bulb; deciduous.
Blooms in spring or summer.

Location: Border, container, greenhouse, house, alpine house, rock garden.

Soil: Most well-drained garden soils.

Care: Water regularly during growth and blooming. No feeding is necessary in most garden soils.

Bearing clusters of starlike white or near white, black- or green-centered flowers, the various ornithogalums make a vivid display when planted in clumps or drifts. Because of their showiness and unusual durability in a vase, they have become staples of the cut flower trade, particularly O. thyrsoides, which is grown under glass for cutting during much of the year. Natives of the Mediterranean area and South Africa, they are similar—and very undemanding—in their needs. Most are regularly available from bulb specialists, and some are occasionally available from general suppliers.

Plant large bulbs in the fall, 4 inches deep and 2 to 5 inches apart, or 1 inch deep in pots or bulb pans, five or six per 6-inch pan. Smaller bulbs should be planted less deep and spaced closer. Propagate them in fall from offsets or from seed planted in the spring.

Ornithogalum arabicum

O. arabicum (star-of-Bethlehem) grows to 2 feet tall and bears clusters of fragrant 1-inch white flowers with shiny black centers. It is hardy to –10° F.

O. caudatum (sea onion), from South Africa, has unshowy flowers but a large, and largely above-ground, bulb that bears numerous bulblets on its surface. This species is popular as a houseplant.

O. nutans also grows to 2 feet tall and bears nodding, 2-inch greenish-white flowers. Where adapted, this species naturalizes in shady woodland conditions.

O. saundersiae (giant chincherinchee), from South Africa, grows to 3 feet or taller and in late summer bears rather flat spikes of many 1-inch flowers with shiny green-black centers. Particularly tender, it must be protected or dug and stored where the ground freezes.

O. thyrsoides (wonder flower, chincherinchee), another South African, grows to about 18 inches tall and bears dense spikes of 1-inch white or cream flowers with brownish green centers. It is particularly prized as a cut flower.

O. umbellatum (like O. arabicum, called star-of-Bethlehem), is native to wide areas of North Africa, Asia Minor, and Europe, and it has naturalized in the southern United States. In the garden it can become invasive. It bears dense spikes of 1-inch white flowers on 1-foot stems.

Oxalis regnellii

Pancratium maritimum

Oxalis

Oxalis family.
Tuber, rhizome, or true bulb; deciduous.
Blooms in various seasons, according to species.

Location: Rock garden, container, house, greenhouse.

Soil: Well drained, sandy, acid to neutral.

Care: Water regularly and provide light to medium feeding with complete fertilizer during growth and blooming; dry off in pot or dig and store cool in dry packing material during dormancy.

Exposure: Sun or light shade.

Irish shamrock is one of this large group of cloverlike plants from various parts of the world. Their great attraction, aside from sometimes variegated shamrock leaves, is their showy, wide-open, funnellike, silky flowers in widely varying colors. Many of the prettiest species can quickly become virtually ineradicable weeds, so container culture is recommended. Species described here make excellent houseplants as well as ornamentals for the garden. These are sometimes offered by bulb specialists.

Plant before dormancy ends, about 1 inch deep and 3 to 6 inches apart, or 8 to 16 per 6-inch pot or bulb pan,
depending on species. Repot and divide when containers become crowded. Propagate from offsets or seeds.

O. adenophylla, from the high elevations of Chile and Argentina, grows to 6 inches tall and bears 1½-inch purple-based lilac-pink flowers in late spring and early summer. It is especially hardy: to –20° F.

O. bowiei, from South Africa, produces 1½-inch pink to rose-purple flowers in the summer. It is effectively grown in hanging baskets.

O. braziliensis, from Brazil, grows to 6 inches or taller and bears 1-inch crimson or rosy purple flowers with darker veins, in late spring and early summer.

O. hirta, from South Africa, grows to 1 foot tall and bears bright purple, rose, violet, white, or yellow flowers on branched stems, in late fall and winter. It may be grown in hanging baskets.

O. pes-caprae, from South Africa, grows 1½-inch bright yellow flowers on foot-high plants. It can become a weed in mild climates.

O. purpurea 'Grand Duchess', from South Africa, has 2-inch pink flowers on 6-inch plants, in fall or winter. It is attractive in hanging baskets.

O. regnellii, from South America, has large shamrock leaves and 1-inch white flowers on plants to 10 inches high. This excellent houseplant can be forced to bloom in any season.

Oxalis pes-caprae

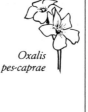

Pancratium maritimum

Pancratium

Amaryllis family.
True bulb; deciduous.
Blooms mid- or late summer.

Location: Border, container, greenhouse, house.

Soil: Well drained, sandy, acid to neutral.

Care: Water generously and feed regularly with a complete fertilizer during period of active growth; then stop feeding and dry off and, where necessary, dig and store.

Exposure: Sun or very light shade.

Almost indistinguishable from its American relative, hymenocallis, this Mediterranean native bears wonderfully fragrant 3-inch flowers in midsummer. Its cultural needs are also virtually identical to those of hymenocallis. See page 71.

Two easily grown species are sometimes available from bulb specialists.

P. illyricum, native to rocky low-altitude places in the Mediterranean area, particularly Corsica, bears 10 to 15 blossoms atop flower stalks 12 to 18 inches tall.

P. maritimum (sea onion), native to the sandy beaches of the Mediterranean, has sparser flowers on 1-foot bloom stalks. Its foliage, unlike that of *P. illyricum* is gray green. It blooms in late summer.

Polianthes tuberosa

Polianthes tuberosa

Tuberose

Agave family.
Tuber; deciduous.
Blooms outdoors summer and fall,
indoors spring or fall.

Location: House, greenhouse, border, container.

Soil: Moist, well drained, organic, acid to neutral.

Care: Water and feed generously during period of growth and blooming.

Exposure: Sun.

So heady is the fragrance of tuberose that some people prefer smelling it in the garden rather than in the confines of the house. Its 2½-inch waxy white flowers are borne on stalks 2 to 3½ feet tall, and they open progressively upward for several weeks. Where the temperatures do not drop below 20° F, this native of Mexico overwinters safely, but farther north it must be container grown or dug and stored over winter. Tuberose is excellent as a cut flower, lasting up to two weeks if the stems are recut periodically.

In the spring after the last frost, plant tubers in the garden, beneath no more than 1 inch of soil and 8 inches apart. Feed and water it regularly. The plant may need staking in windy spots. Check frequently for aphids, which damage buds and stunt growth. Where it is not hardy, dig up the tuber after the foliage is dead and store it in a dry place in sawdust, sand, or peat moss at no lower than 60° F. For container culture indoors or in the greenhouse, plant one tuber per 5-inch pot and keep the air temperature at 75° F or higher with a humid atmosphere in winter for spring blooming, or in late summer for fall blooming.

Puschkinia scilloides

Puschkinia scilloides

Striped squill

Lily family.
True bulb; deciduous.
Blooms late winter or early spring.

Location: Rock garden, meadow, alpine house.

Soil: Well drained, sandy, acid to neutral.

Care: Water regularly during growth and flowering. Little or no fertilizing is needed.

Exposure: Sun or light shade.

Native to Asia Minor and the Caucasus, *Puschkinia scilloides* is similar to the chionodoxas and many of the scillas. Hardy to –30° F, puschkinia grows well where the ground freezes. It looks best naturalized in clumps and drifts. Its 6-inch spikes of bluish white, blue-striped flowers rise from among 6-inch straplike leaves. Solid blue and white forms are sometimes sold. The plant sometimes sold as *P. libanotica* (Lebanon squill) is a pale blue, pale-striped variety of *P. scilloides*. Puschkinia is widely available.

Plant bulbs 3 inches deep and 3 inches apart, in fall. Propagate in the fall from offsets. Do not dig and divide puschkinia unnecessarily.

Ranunculus asiaticus

Ranunculus asiaticus

Persian buttercup

Buttercup family.
Tuberous roots; deciduous.
Blooms in spring.

Location: Border, container, greenhouse, alpine house.

Soil: Well drained, sandy, acid to neutral.

Care: Water regularly and feed lightly during growth and flowering; dry off during summer and fall dormancy; where not hardy, dig and store warm in dry packing material.

Exposure: Sun to partial shade.

Magnificently full, double, 3- to 5-inch flowers whose colors include white and shades of red, pink, orange, gold, and bronze make the 12- to 18-inch-tall ranunculus a favorite in the cut-flower trade and in the garden. It is ideally suited for growth as a perennial in mild-winter, dry-summer areas. Elsewhere it can be grown with seasonal digging and storing. A single clawlike tuberous root produces dozens of flowers in a season. Hybrid strains are widely sold.

Where the winter temperatures do not drop below 0° F, plant in the fall; farther north, plant in the spring. If the tuberous roots are very dry and shriveled, soak them for a few hours in water or place them in moist sand for a few days before planting. Plant tuberous roots with the prongs pointing downward, 4 inches deep and 4 inches apart in the garden or 1-inch deep in a pot, one per 6-inch pot. Dormant ranunculus are more difficult to store successfully than most bulbs, so many gardeners purchase fresh tubers at the start of each season.

Polianthes
tuberosa

Puschkinia
scilloides

Ranunculus
asiaticus

Rhodohypoxis baurii

Rhodohypoxis baurii

Hypoxis family.
Corm; deciduous.
Blooms in summer.

Location: Rock garden, border, container, alpine house.

Soil: Fast draining, sandy, acid to neutral.

Care: Water generously during spring and summer growth and blooming; reduce or stop watering during winter dormancy. Little or no feeding is necessary in most soils.

Exposure: Sun.

Rhodohypoxis baurii

From the high-altitude areas of South Africa and Lesotho comes this diminutive plant with numerous upward-facing, 1½-inch flowers in white or shades of pink, rose, rose-red, and red and grasslike foliage with silky hairs. It is only 3 or 4 inches high and can be used effectively in sink gardens, chinks of a dry wall, and spaces between paving stones. It is hardy to 10° F. A few specialists are beginning to offer it.

Plant corms 1 to 2 inches deep and 2 to 3 inches apart. Propagate by division, not during dormancy but during the period of growth.

Rigidella orthantha

Rigidella orthantha

Iris family.
True bulb; semievergreen.
Blooms in summer.

Location: Greenhouse, container, border.

Soil: Fast draining, sandy, organic, acid to neutral.

Care: Water generously and feed lightly with complete fertilizer during period of growth and blooming; reduce watering and stop feeding during fall and winter.

Exposure: Broken sunlight to light shade.

From the high-altitude cloud forests of Guatemala and Mexico comes this close relative of tigridia, which bears brilliant scarlet flowers with recurved petals and prominent orange-yellow filaments. Its erect bloom stems grow to 3 feet tall.

In early spring, plant the bulbs 3 inches deep in a cool place, and water lightly until growth begins. Then grow them at warm temperatures. If necessary, stake the stems as they elongate. After flowering has ended, reduce watering, and protect them from heavy rainfall during the winter. Where they are not hardy, grow them in containers, store the containers cool, and water them occasionally during storage to keep soil slightly moist. Propagate by offsets in late fall.

R. orthantha is only occasionally offered by some specialists. *R. flammea*, with clusters of nodding scarlet flowers, is also difficult to locate, as are hybrids between *R. orthantha* and *Tigridia pavonia*.

Rigidella orthantha

Romulea bulbocodium

Romulea amoena

Romulea

Iris family.
Corm; deciduous.
Blooms late winter until hot weather.

Location: Rock garden, border, container, alpine house.

Soil: Well drained, organic, sandy, acid to neutral.

Care: Water generously during period of active growth, starting in fall; dry off during dormancy. In most soils, little or no fertilizing is needed.

Exposure: Sun.

Romuleas come from the wet-winter areas of South Africa and the Mediterranean area. They are related to crocuses but have a wider color range. Flowers emerge from corms singly or in clusters and stay open only in bright sunlight. The undersides of the petals of many species are beautifully feathered, as are those of many crocuses. Most thrive in rock gardens and outdoor containers in mild-winter, dry-summer areas like California. South African species are frost tender, but most Mediterranean species are nearly as hardy as crocuses. A few South African species, not described here, require summer wetness and drying off during winter. Romulea bulbs may be hard to locate but are worth the search.

Plant corms in the fall, before their growing season begins. Use informal clumps or small drifts, with corms planted 3 inches deep and 3 inches apart. In a 6-inch bulb pan plant five or six corms 2 inches deep. Repot when plants become crowded. Propagate by seeds during cool weather, keeping the medium moist until seeds have germinated, in about two months.

The three Mediterranean species that follow are particularly attractive.

Scadoxus multiflorus

Schizostylis coccinea 'Sunrise'

R. bulbocodium usually has 1¼-inch yellow- or white-throated lilac flowers with purple veining on the undersides, though coloration is variable. It needs some protection from heavy spring rains.

R. clusiana, similar to *R. bulbocodium*, has slightly larger flowers.

R. grandiscapa has deep violet flowers.

Among the multitude of beautiful South African romuleas, you might try to locate the following.

R. amoena, one of the most extravagantly beautiful species, has large, deep red flowers with six-point black stars at their centers, and fine black lines radiating outward through a pale yellow, black-edged throat.

R. atrandra has deep pink flowers with dark blotches around pale yellow centers. Some forms also have deep purple markings.

R. obscura var. *campestris* has flowers varying from pale to rich orange, or an apricot cast.

R. rosea has reddish lilac to rose pink flowers with yellow throats. Each of the three outer petals has three purple stripes on the outside.

R. sabulosa, like *R. amoena*, has large flowers, to 4 inches wide, with a satiny sheen. The color varies from old rose to red, and the petals are delicately veined in a slightly deeper tone. At the base of each petal is an oblong blotch, black on top and yellow underneath.

R. tortuosa has big, bright yellow flowers with deep purple brown blotches surrounding pale yellow centers, and a clove scent.

Scadoxus multiflorus subspecies katharinae

(Haemanthus katharinae)

Amaryllis family.
True bulb; deciduous.
Blooms late spring, summer, or fall.

Location: Container, greenhouse, house.

Soil: Fast draining, organic, acid to neutral.

Care: Water regularly and feed lightly during active growth, reduce watering or dry off and store warm in pots during winter dormancy.

Exposure: Light shade; medium shade in hot climates.

This native of South African woodlands bears spectacular, large, dense umbels of scarlet to salmon-red flowers, each atop a sturdy, succulent stem 1 to 2 feet tall. Umbels are usually 5 to 6 inches in diameter but may be as large as 9 inches. You can buy scadoxus from some specialists and occasionally from a general supplier.

In the spring plant bulbs with their tops exposed, one bulb per pot twice its circumference. Household temperatures are sufficient during growth and blooming. With mulching, scadoxus usually overwinters well where temperatures get no lower than 20° F. Leave it undisturbed for as long as possible. Propagate from offsets in spring during repotting or replanting.

Scadoxus multiflorus subspecies katharinae

Schizostylis coccinea

Schizostylis coccinea

Crimson flag, Kaffir lily

Iris family.
Rhizome; semievergreen.
Blooms in fall.

Location: Border, container, greenhouse, alpine house.

Soil: Organic, acid to neutral.

Care: Provide ample water during summer and fall period of growth and flowering, then reduce watering somewhat. Feed lightly with complete fertilizer during growth.

Exposure: Sun or partial shade.

Its 6 to 12 silky crimson flowers, 2½ inches wide per slender 2-foot spike, together with swordlike narrow green leaves, make this native of the rich, dark-soiled riversides in South Africa one of the showiest bulbs for garden, container, or vase. It grows particularly well in humid environments, quickly forming large clumps. *Schizostylis* is hardy to 0° F. It is becoming available from specialists and a few general suppliers. Named varieties are sold occasionally, including 'Mrs. Hegarty', with pale pink flowers, and 'Sunrise', with large pink flowers.

Plant or divide rhizomes in the fall, just after the flowering period, or in the spring. Set the rhizomes 1 to 2 inches deep. Regular watering during growth and blooming is essential.

Scilla siberica

Scilla

Squill

Lily family.
True bulb; deciduous.
Blooms in late winter or spring.

Cultural needs and garden uses of most scillas are the same as for *Hyacinthoides*. See page 71.

Deprived of its former bluebell species—now called *Hyacinthoides* (*Endymion*)—the genus *Scilla* still includes some very special spring garden bulbs for naturalistic plantings, container growth, and cutting. All species listed here are widely available.

S. bifolia, from Europe and southwestern Asia, grows to 6 inches high and bears blue flowers very early in the spring. Rose and white forms are also sold.

S. peruviana (Cuban lily), from neither Peru nor Cuba but the Mediterranean area, has wide, glossy, straplike leaves and in late spring bears slightly pointed domes of bluish purple flowers on 10- to 18-inch stems. Dormancy is brief. Plant bulbs close to the surface of the soil, in sun. For container culture, plant one per 6-inch pot.

S. siberica (Siberian squill) is particularly hardy because, as its name implies, it is from Siberia. It bears deep blue flowers on 6-inch spikes very early in the spring. Other color forms are sometimes sold. 'Spring Beauty', very deep blue and taller than the species, is a choice variety.

S. tubergeniana is an Iranian squill bearing delicately pale blue flowers with darker stripes down the petals. It also blooms early.

Sinningia speciosa

Gloxinia

Gesneria family.
Tuber; deciduous.
Blooms in any season, after cyclical dormancy, up to twice a year.

Location: House, greenhouse, container seasonally outdoors.

Soil: Well drained, organic, acid to neutral.

Care: During active growth and blooming, water regularly and feed with diluted complete fertilizer. Five or six weeks after blooming, when leaves begin to die back, dry off gradually and store cool with soil barely moist for several months until sprouting starts. Then gradually resume regular watering and feeding.

Exposure: Filtered light, as for its cousin, African violet, or artificial light.

From the forest floors of Brazil comes this plant sold as a flowering potted plant by florists everywhere, and as seeds or dormant tubers by some general suppliers and specialists. Flowers of unhybridized forms are quietly lovely, but florists' hybrids are spectacular 1-foot plants with broad, fuzzy leaves 4 to 6 inches long, and upright, bell-shaped, 3- to 6-inch flowers with scalloped, ruffled edges, single- or bicolored in shades of purple, violet, red, pink, rose, and white, often finely edged or spotted. Some forms have slipper-shaped flowers or nodding tubular ones, and certain hybrids are diminutive. Some recently developed hybrids between *Sinningia* and other gesneriads are evergreen and everblooming.

Plant one *S. speciosa* tuber per pot, sprouted side of the tuber up, in a pot about 3 inches greater in diameter than the tuber. Cover with no more than 1 inch of soil. During the growing period, keep the soil moist and the surrounding humidity high (easily done by placing the pot on a tray of moist pebbles, but not standing in water). If more than one shoot appears, remove all but the most vigorous one. During dormancy, store at about 60° F in a dark, humid place. Afterward, repot the tuber in fresh houseplant or African violet soil mix. Propagate by dividing the tuber as for tuberous begonia (see page 31), by rooting leaf cuttings or sprouts in moist sand, or by sowing seeds on top of moist peat moss in a warm, humid, bright place.

Scilla bifolia

Sinningia speciosa

Smithiantha exoniensis

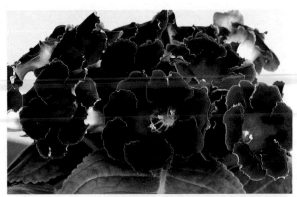

Sinningia speciosa

Smithiantha × zebrina 'Carmel'

Smithiantha

(*Naegelia*)
Temple bells

Gesneria family.
Scaly rhizome; deciduous.
Blooms late summer or fall to midwinter.

Cultural requirements of *Smithiantha* are identical to those of the closely related *Sinningia speciosa*.

Native to tropical, moist regions of Mexico, smithiantha has spikes of bright, gracefully nodding tubular flowers with flared, lobed tips, borne on upright stems. Smithiantha is offered occasionally by specialists, florists, and houseplant shops.

S. cinnabarina grows 1 to 2 feet tall. It has deep-green leaves up to 6 inches long and 5 inches wide with purple veins and reddish hairs on the tops and pale green undersides variegated with purple. The 1½-inch flowers are brick-red banded with pale yellow or white on their low parts and outsides, with red lips marked by cream lines and spots.

S. zebrina grows to 2½ feet tall and has dark green, purple-variegated leaves and scarlet flowers with yellow and orange markings.

Sparaxis tricolor

Spiloxene capensis

Sparaxis

Harlequin flower

Iris family.
Corm; deciduous.
Blooms spring or early summer.

Location: Rock garden, border, alpine house, container.

Soil: Well drained, sandy, neutral to alkaline.

Care: Water after weather cools in autumn, through winter and spring; then dry off, or dig and store, until cool fall weather. Little or no fertilizing necessary in good garden soils.

Exposure: Sun.

Harlequin flower, including the species formerly classified separately as *Streptanthera*, is as dazzling and colorful as its name implies. Clusters of kaleidoscope-like patterned and colored flowers up to 2 inches wide bloom atop 6- to 24-inch stems. It is hardy outdoors to 20° F; elsewhere it can be grown under glass.

In the rock garden or border, plant corms 4 inches deep and 4 inches apart, in early fall. Remove mulch when sprouts appear. Taller stems may require staking. Allow soil to dry out through the summer and into fall. For container culture outdoors or in the alpine house, plant five or six corms per 6-inch pot. After blooming, store the containers in a sunny, dry spot and allow the soil to dry out. (This is easily done anywhere if you turn pots on their sides.) Repot in fresh soil the following fall. Propagate in the fall from cormlets.

S. elegans (formerly *Streptanthera cuprea* and *elegans*) has white flowers, marked in their throats with narrow brownish bars edged with a flush of salmon. Another form is vermilion fading to pink, with violet and yellow markings often creating a striking geometric pattern. *S. elegans* is available through many specialists.

S. grandiflora is variable, with golden yellow, cream, deep violet, white stained with violet, or deep purple and yellow flowers. It is available through many specialists.

S. tricolor, the most popular species, is widely available in a multitude of color combinations, including some named varieties like 'Fire King'. A typical *S. tricolor* blossom is either vermilion or salmon marked with black or red. A number of brilliant-colored hybrids with a variety of markings are sold under this name.

Sparaxis tricolor

Spiloxene capensis

Spiloxene capensis

Hypoxis family.
Corm; deciduous.
Blooms late winter to early spring in garden, earlier indoors.

Location: Container, rock garden, alpine house.

Soil: Well drained, acid to neutral.

Care: Water regularly during period of growth, in winter and spring; dry off completely during summer and early fall. No feeding is necessary in most soils. Dig and store garden-grown corms in wet-summer areas.

Exposure: Sun.

From the wet-winter areas of South Africa comes this lovely but rarely sold plant with neat, grasslike foliage and 6- to 12-inch stems of striking, starlike, 1- to 2½-inch-wide flowers. Colors and markings are as variable as flower size. Common forms are pure yellow, yellow with a brown or khaki eye, and white or pale pink with a green eye and purple markings. Flowers open only during midday, for four or five hours; in South Africa, a common name for this flower is midday stars.

Plant corms in early fall, 3 inches deep and 3 inches apart in the garden where the temperature doesn't drop below 0° F, or 1 inch deep and three per 6-inch pot. Propagate in the fall from offsets.

Sprekelia formosissima

Sprekelia formosissima

(*Amaryllis formosissima*)
Aztec lily, Jacobean lily,
St. James's lily

Amaryllis family.
True bulb; deciduous.
Blooms in spring and summer.

Location: House, greenhouse, container, border.

Soil: Fast draining, organic, sandy, acid to neutral.

Care: Feed with balanced fertilizer and water regularly except during dormancy.

Exposure: Sun.

The spectacular 5-inch crimson flowers of the Aztec lily, borne singly on 12- to 15-inch stems, are orchidlike in form and texture. The foliage is dark, narrow, and straplike. This native of Mexico, like its close cousin, hippeastrum, makes an excellent container plant for a bright window, and it thrives in sunny, hot spots outdoors where the temperature does not drop below 10° F. In such climates plant it in the fall, 4 inches deep and 8 to 12 inches apart. Elsewhere plant it in the spring, let it go dry after flowering, and dig and store the bulb in sand, peat moss, or sawdust in a cool spot for the winter. For greenhouse or house culture, plant in early fall in a small (3- to 5-inch) pot, with the neck of the bulb above soil level. Treat it like hippeastrum (see page 70). Repot it every three or four years, propagating by division.

Sprekelia is widely sold.

Sternbergia lutea

Sprekelia formosissima

Sternbergia lutea

Lily-of-the-field

Amaryllis family.
True bulb; deciduous.
Blooms in fall.

Location: Rock garden, container, alpine house.

Soil: Very fast draining, neutral to alkaline; gritty rock garden soil is ideal.

Care: Water regularly during growth and blooming; dry off over summer. Little or no feeding is necessary.

Exposure: Sun.

In the fall, the golden yellow, crocuslike, 1½-inch-long flowers (four or five per bulb) of sternbergia appear on stems to 6 inches high. Attractive linear leaves appear with or after flowers. This native of the Mediterranean area and central Asia often blooms along with *Crocus speciosus*. It is available from specialists and occasionally from some general suppliers. 'Major', which has larger flowers, is sometimes sold.

Plant the bulbs in the summer, 4 inches deep and 4 to 6 inches apart in the sunniest, warmest part of your garden, and leave them undisturbed; disturbed bulbs usually do not bloom the following year. Or plant them 2 inches deep in a bulb pan, five per 6-inch pan, and leave them in the pan for several years. Propagate them in the summer from offsets.

*Sternbergia
lutea*

*Tecophilaea
cyanocrocus*

Tecophilaea cyanocrocus 'Violacea'

Streptanthera

See *Sparaxis*, page 87.

Tecophilaea cyanocrocus

Chilean crocus

Tecophilaea family.
Corm; deciduous.
Blooms in early spring.

Location: Rock garden, container, alpine house, greenhouse.

Soil: Fast draining, sandy, acid to neutral.

Care: Water regularly during the brief growing period in late winter until after flowering, then dry off in garden or pot, in hot, sunny place. Very light feeding is beneficial after sprout is well developed.

Exposure: Sun.

This crocuslike native of the stony Andean slopes produces perfumed, gentian blue flowers that have no rival for beauty among the little bulbs. Sadly, it has been collected and grazed out of existence in the wild, so it is a particular treasure for bulb collectors. The flowers, one to three per plant, are held up to 6 inches high. Tecophilaea is hardy to 10° F. It is occasionally sold by specialists. Varieties 'Leichtlinii' (paler flowers with white centers) and 'Violacea' (intense violet blue flowers) are also sold.

In late summer or fall, plant corms 5 inches deep and 4 inches apart in the garden, or 2 inches deep in a pot, two or three per 5-inch pot. Mulch the soil in the winter until sprouting begins, and protect bulbs from too much winter rain. Because the corms are extremely expensive, Chilean crocus is often grown only in containers, even in areas where it will grow outdoors.

Tigridia pavonia

Tigridia pavonia

Tiger flower, Mexican shell flower

Iris family.
True bulb; deciduous.
Blooms in summer.

Location: Greenhouse, alpine house, container, border.

Soil: Fast draining, sandy, organic, acid to neutral.

Care: Water generously and feed lightly with complete fertilizer during period of growth and blooming; stop watering and feeding during fall and winter.

Exposure: Sun or some light shade in hot climates.

Brilliantly colored blossoms of white to pink, red, purple, orange, and yellow, usually with con- trasting spotting around the center of the flower, make tigridia one of the showiest bulbs. Where well adapted in gardens that get no colder than 0° F, it sometimes naturalizes by reseeding. A fan of pleated leaves adds to its attractiveness in borders or containers, and its scale—3- to 6-inch flowers borne profusely on stems to 2 feet tall—makes it imposing wherever you situate it. Each flower lasts only a day, but tigridia blooms heavily over many weeks.

In spring (or earlier indoors, if you wish) plant bulbs 3 inches deep in a cool spot, water lightly until growth commences, and grow at warm temperatures. Use stakes for support if necessary. After flowering, reduce and then stop watering. Where

tigridia is adapted to winter temperatures, you can mulch over the bulbs and leave them in the ground; elsewhere, dig and store the bulbs in sawdust, peat moss, or sand; or store containers in a cold, dry place. Propagate by offsets in the fall. Seeds are easy to start in the spring, either indoors or in the ground.

Tigridia is widely sold, by general suppliers as well as specialists. Named color selections as well as seed mixes are available.

Trillium

Wake-robin

Lily family.
Rhizome; deciduous.
Blooms in spring.

Location: Woodland, shady border.

Soil: Cool, well drained, organic, acid to neutral.

Care: Water regularly the year around; little or no feeding is necessary in rich woodland soil.

Exposure: Light to medium shade.

Among the love- liest spring woodland flowers in North America and parts of Asia, trilliums form clumps of beautiful foliage that, in most species, last through the summer. Each stem bears a whorl of three leaves, handsomely mottled in some species, and three showy petals backed by three less-showy segments. Most species thrive in the United States wherever the ground freezes in the winter. Where well adapted, clumps increase slowly by spreading from deep rhizomes to create small-to moderate-sized areas of ground cover. Trilliums look best with other woodland plants such as arisaemas and ferns. You can buy tubers of the common species from general suppliers as well as specialists; seeds or tubers of less common species are offered occasionally by specialists.

In the fall plant rhizomes 2 to 4 inches deep and 4 to 8 inches apart. Undisturbed clumps will enlarge and endure for many years. Propagate by division in the fall, or by sowing newly ripened, fresh seeds in a cold frame where there will be alternate freezing and thawing during winter.

T. chloropetalum, native from Washington to central California, grows 2 to 2½ feet high and bears flowers varying in color from rich

Trillium chloropetalum

mahogany to pink or white. The leaves are mottled.

T. erectum (purple trillium), from eastern North America, bears maroon, purple, or brownish purple, sometimes white, yellow, or green flowers atop 2-foot-tall plants.

T. grandiflorum (white wake-robin), from eastern North America, bears white flowers that turn rosy pink with age. It grows 1 to 1½ feet tall.

T. sessile (toadshade) grows to 1 foot tall, and has maroon, brownish purple, or greenish flowers. Leaves are often mottled. It is native to the eastern United States.

Triteleia

See *Brodiaea*, page 45.

Tigridia pavonia

Trillium ovatum

Tritonia

Iris family.
Corm; deciduous.
Blooms spring or summer in garden, spring in greenhouse.

Location: Border, rock garden, container, alpine house.

Soil: Any well-drained, rich garden soil.

Care: Water and feed with a complete fertilizer regularly during winter to spring or summer growth and blooming, then keep dry until the next growing season. No fertilizing necessary in garden soil.

Exposure: Sun.

Closely allied with crocosmia, some species of tritonia called montebretia look virtually identical to the more-common crocosmia species also called montebretia. More distinctive are two smaller, softer-looking, but very showy tritonia species. Both are excellent cut flowers, lasting a week or longer.

Where the winters do not get colder than 0° F, and where they can be kept dry during their late summer and fall dormancy, plant the corms in the spring or the fall to remain in the ground the year around. Where winters are colder than 0° F, plant after the last frost, setting the corms 3 to 4 inches deep and as far apart. After blooming, dry off, dig, and store corms without packing material. For greenhouse container culture, plant five to seven corms per 6-inch pot, 1 inch deep, in the fall; water very sparingly for about a month, then water and feed regularly. When the leaves wither after the spring flowering, set the pots outdoors in full sun and allow them to dry off. Repot in the fall. Propagation is easy from offsets, which are plentiful.

T. *crocata* grows 8 to 18 inches tall and has cup-shaped, 1½- to 2-inch flowers on spikes held above fans of narrow, bladelike foliage. A multitude of named hybrids are sold. Colors include white, amber shaded with pink, deep orange, soft pink, soft salmon, salmon orange, and cream with yellow centers.

T. *hyalina*, classified by some botanists as a form of T. *crocata*, is similar in size and form. It bears orange or salmon flowers with translucent bases.

Tritonia crocata

Tulbaghia

Allium family.
Bulb; evergreen.
Blooms in any season.

Location: Container, border, house, greenhouse.

Soil: Any well-drained garden soil.

Care: Undemanding, but it's best to water regularly. Little or no feeding is necessary in most garden soils.

Exposure: Sun.

As a garden plant where winters do not get colder than 20° F, a container plant brought indoors during winter in more northerly areas, or a houseplant anywhere, tulbaghia offers an extraordinarily long season of blooming. Both available species are from the mild-climate areas of South Africa.

Plant tubers in the garden 1 to 2 inches deep, 8 to 12 inches apart, in any season. Clumps grow rather quickly. Divide container-grown plants when they become crowded. Propagate by division or offsets.

T. *fragrans* (sweet garlic) bears dense umbels of ¾-inch, sweet-scented, bright lilac flowers on stems 12 to 18 inches long above arching 12-inch leaves. In the garden it blooms during the winter and spring. It makes an excellent cut flower, lasting more than a week.

T. *violacea* (society garlic), available from some specialists and occasionally from general nurseries, bears sparser umbels of ¾-inch, bright lilac flowers on 1- to 2½-foot stems, mainly in the spring and summer. It is a useful culinary herb that can be substituted for chives, but bruised or cut tissue has an oniony odor, which makes it less popular as a cut flower.

Tulbaghia fragrans

Tritonia hyalina

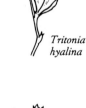

Tulbaghia violacea

Tulipa eichleri

Tulipa

Tulip
Lily family.
True bulb; deciduous.
Blooms in spring.

Location: Border and bed, container, house, greenhouse.

Soil: Well drained, deep, organic.

Care: Water regularly during growth and blooming. Mix a teaspoon of bonemeal or sewage sludge in the soil at the bottom of each planting hole, or spread 1 cup per square yard when planting; feed again with complete fertilizer when sprouts emerge from the ground.

Exposure: Sun or some light shade, especially where summers are hot.

The most celebrated bulbs in the world, garden tulips have a long and fascinating history. Since the introduction of their ancestors into northern Europe from Asia and Asia Minor (where some had been cultivated for centuries) in the sixteenth century, tulips have been admired, grown, and valued over increasingly broad areas of the world.

Garden tulips can be grown easily wherever winters get at least as cold as 20° F, and—with a little more effort—anywhere. They should be planted in the fall—early in the north and late in the south—6 to 8 inches deep and 3 to 6 inches apart. In the South precooled bulbs can be purchased (see page 20). Most garden tulips are vigorous and free blooming only in their first year and are usually replaced annually, especially in formal plantings. (See page 13.) However, if you select the proper varieties and plant them deep (up to 8 inches) and in mild-winter areas dig and

Parrot tulip 'Texas Flame'

Tulipa kaufmanniana 'Honorose'

Veltheimia bracteata

refrigerate them at 35° to 50° F through the heat of summer and early fall (but without drying the bulbs out), you can maintain them for several years. A newly developed class marketed as perennial tulips are satisfactory for long-term cultivation, even for naturalizing. Protect tulip bulbs in the garden from rodents, which are particularly fond of them. Propagate, when practicable, from offsets. Tulips are superlative cut flowers, lasting six to eight days, but the stems sometimes elongate, twist, and reach toward the light.

Tulips are spectacular container plants indoors or out. Early-blooming varieties can be forced by planting six or seven bulbs in a 6-inch pot or bulb pan with the tips even with the rim of the container. See page 20.

The following are the current classes of garden tulips, according to the *Classified List of Tulip Names*, published by the Royal Bulb Growers' Association, Hillegom, The Netherlands.

Early flowering:

1. Single Early Tulips, generally 10 to 14 inches tall, with large flowers.

2. Double Early Tulips, 10 to 12 inches tall, up to 4 inches across.

Midseason flowering:

3. Triumph Tulips, hybrids of early- and late-flowering types, average height 12 to 14 inches.

4. Darwin Hybrid Tulips, some of the largest-flowered and most brilliant tulips, 18 to 24 inches tall.

Late flowering:

5. Single Late Tulips (including Darwin and Cottage Tulips), up to 30 inches tall.

6. Lily-Flowered Tulips, usually 16 to 18 inches tall with pointed petals turned outward at the tips.

7. Fringed Tulips, finely fringed petals, variable in height.

8. Viridiflora Tulips, also variable in height, with partly green blossoms.

9. Rembrandt Tulips, with variegated flowers; variable height.

10. Parrot Tulips, bicolored flowers with twisted, irregularly fringed petals, stems 16 to 18 inches tall.

11. Double Late Tulips, long-lasting flowers whose shape gives them the name "peony flowered," to about 14 inches tall.

Species Tulips:

Location: Rock garden, border, container, house, alpine house.

Soil: For most, any well-drained soil.

Care: Water regularly through winter until flowering, then dry off and in wet-summer areas, store at 65° F or above until planting time; fertilize as for garden tulips, but lightly.

Exposure: Sun.

These beautiful, often diminutive plants (6 to 11 inches) are prized by knowledgeable gardeners, who plant bulbs deep to duplicate the natural growing situation (baking, dry summers and cool, rainy winters for most) for best results. Where adapted, many tulip species naturalize, even in a bulb frame.

The following are a few generally available species tulips.

T. kaufmanniana varieties and hybrids (water-lily tulip) with pointed-petaled, wide-open flowers, 4- to 8-inch stems, early blooming.

T. fosteriana varieties and hybrids, bearing flowers up to 8 inches wide on 8- to 20-inch stems; long-lived in gardens where adapted.

T. greigii varieties and hybrids, 10 to 14 inches high, midseason bloomers with large blossoms and handsome, maroon striped and mottled low foliage.

Vallota speciosa

See *Cyrtanthus purpureus,* page 56.

Veltheimia bracteata

(V. viridifolia)
Lily family.
True bulb; deciduous.
Blooms in winter or early spring.

Location: Border, greenhouse, house, alpine house, container.

Soil: Well drained, sandy, acid to neutral.

Care: Water regularly and feed occasionally with complete fertilizer during period of growth from fall to spring; dry off or reduce watering and stop feeding during summer.

Exposure: Light shade.

Rosettes of wavy-edged, glossy, deep green leaves; dappled 1- to 1½-foot bloom stems, and dense clusters of drooping tubular flowers, typically pinkish red or pinkish purple with green and white flecks, make this native of South African coastal forests one of the handsomest bulbs for container culture. It is hardy outdoors in well-protected locations where the winter doesn't get colder than 10° F. There is some confusion among suppliers over proper designations of veltheimia species; nearly all of the ones available (from specialists) are probably forms of *V. bracteata*.

In the fall plant each bulb with the top one third exposed. Keep the soil evenly moist, and in the spring, propagate from offsets.

Veltheimia bracteata

Watsonia beatricis

Worsleya rayneri

Watsonia

Bugle lily

Iris family.
Corm; deciduous or evergreen, depending on species.
Blooms early spring through summer, depending on species.

Cultural requirements and garden uses are the same as for winter-growing gladiolus. See page 65.

Like most of its gladiolus cousins, watsonia is a stately South African garden flower that in most climate areas requires digging and storing over winter. Evergreen species can be treated as deciduous ones: Dried off and dug as necessary. It is a superlative cut flower, airier and more loosely graceful than its stiffer, larger-flowered cousin. A number of species are occasionally sold by some specialists and general suppliers, together with an increasing number of hybrids. Where adapted to garden cultivation, it looks best when allowed to develop substantial clumps.

Some watsonias are imposing in scale, and others are small enough to grow as houseplants or to use in small outdoor containers and near fronts of borders.

Among the smaller species, all around 18 inches tall, are W. brevifolia (pink to rosy pink flowers), W. coccinea (scarlet flowers), and W. meriana (variable, often bright red flowers, evergreen, remarkably long blooming).

Among the many larger watsonias are the following.

W. angusta (W. fulgens), a moisture lover, grows to 3 feet and has scarlet flowers with violet anthers.

W. beatricis is 3 to 4 feet high and evergreen and has pink-tipped apricot flowers.

W. fourcadei grows up to 5 feet tall and bears branched spikes of flowers that vary in color but are often brick red with purple anthers on pale pink filaments.

W. marginata grows 4 to 5 feet tall, bears cup-shaped flowers that are lilac marked with magenta and white and has bluish green leaves with yellowish edges.

W. pyramidata grows to 5½ feet tall, has branched spikes of mauvish pink flowers with brownish purple anthers, and is very early blooming.

Watsonia
rosea

Worsleya
rayneri

Worsleya rayneri

Blue amaryllis

Amaryllis family.
True bulb; evergreen.
Blooms spring or summer.

Location: Greenhouse, house, border in frost-free areas.

Soil: Fast draining, organic, acid to neutral.

Care: Water regularly; stop feeding and reduce water during dormancy, October to December.

Exposure: Full sun.

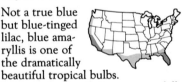

Not a true blue but blue-tinged lilac, blue amaryllis is one of the dramatically beautiful tropical bulbs. In its native Brazil, it grows on cliff ledges. It bears 6 to 10 white-based, amethyst-flecked, 5½- to 6½-inch flowers atop a 16-inch stem. Its bold strap leaves, 3 inches wide and to 3 feet long, and gracefully arching, are decorative throughout the year. It is especially well adapted to garden culture in southern Florida, but it must be grown as a house or greenhouse plant in most parts of the country.

Position the large bulb with only its bottom third buried in the soil, in a humid spot where night temperatures are 55° or 60° F. Propagate by division, or sow seeds indoors in any season in a medium kept at 70° to 75° F during the 30-day germination period.

Blue amaryllis is often difficult to locate. It is occasionally sold by specialists.

Zantedeschia aethiopica

Zantedeschia aethiopica

Calla

Arum family.
Rhizome; semideciduous.
Blooms early spring to early summer; sometimes other seasons as well under greenhouse conditions.

Location: Border, container, greenhouse, house.

Soil: Any garden soil; very organic is best.

Care: Water generously and feed monthly during period of growth and blooming; afterward either reduce water or, where not hardy, dry off, dig, and store in dry packing material.

Exposure: Sun or partial shade, especially in hot climates.

The calla—a favorite subject of many artists, an important art deco motif, and a dramatic and popular cut flower—is one of the most familiar flowers, even to people who have seldom seen it growing. Its elegantly tapered and curved white spathe encloses the pale golden spadix that bears the actual flower parts. Its leaves are large, glossy, and deep green. This African native naturalizes in mild areas where it is well adapted, especially in moist or boggy spots. Under such conditions it reaches a

Zephyranthes candida

height of 3 or 4 feet. Several occasionally sold diminutive forms of *Z. aethiopica* are more suitable for pot culture.

Plant rhizomes 4 inches deep and 1 to 2 feet apart in the garden, or 3 inches deep in pots, one per 6-inch pot.

You may find other species and New Zealand hybrids, most of them smaller plants than *Z. aethiopica*, and ranging in color from white or white with purple spots to cream, yellow, gold, bronze, rose, pink, green, red, purple, and bicolors. Many have white- or translucent-spotted leaves. All of these require good drainage and drying off after blooming.

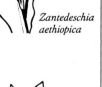

*Zantedeschia
aethiopica*

*Zephyranthes
candida*

Zephyranthes

Zephyr lily, Rain lily, Fairy lily
Amaryllis family.
True bulb; deciduous or evergreen, depending on species and climate. Blooms in summer and fall, sometimes other seasons as well.

Location: Border, rock garden, meadow, container, house.

Soil: Well drained, sandy, acid to neutral.

Care: Alternate periods of watering and drying off to stimulate blooming; dry off for 10 weeks after foliage dies back. No feeding is necessary in most garden soils.

Exposure: Sun.

Appearing suddenly after a rain, typically late in the gardening season, zephyranthes blossoms refresh baked, tired garden landscapes. This tropical American native is equally effective as a container plant, blooming periodically indoors (but set outside during summer) or out. Its solitary, upright blossoms in white or shades of pink, rose, or salmon are held about a foot above tufts of grassy foliage. With protection most species are hardy to 0° F. Zephyranthes are frequently offered by specialists.

Plant bulbs in the garden in the fall where they are hardy, or in the spring elsewhere, 1 to 2 inches deep and 3 to 4 inches apart. Where the bulbs are not hardy, dig them in the fall and store them warm in dry packing material. Plant 10 or 12 bulbs per 6-inch pot, 2 inches deep. Propagate them from offsets.

Z. atamasco (Atamasco lily), from the southeastern United States, bears white or purple-tinged, lilylike, 4-inch flowers on 8- to 12-inch stems. The bulbs are poisonous.

Z. candida, from South America, bears crocuslike, 2-inch white flowers—sometimes brushed with rose on the outsides of the petals—on 1-foot stems.

Z. citrina, another South American, bears bright golden yellow flowers and in all other ways is quite similar to *Z. candida*.

Z. grandiflora (*Z. carinata*), from the moist woodlands of Mexico and Guatemala, grows to 1 foot tall and bears 2½-inch bright pink flowers.

Z. rosea, from the West Indies and Guatemala, bears 1-inch, rose-red flowers on stems up to 1 foot tall.

U.S. MEASURE AND METRIC MEASURE CONVERSION CHART

	Formulas for Exact Measures				Rounded Measures for Quick Reference		
	Symbol	**When you know:**	**Multiply by**	**To find:**			
Mass (Weight)	oz	ounces	28.35	grams	1 oz		= 30 g
	lb	pounds	0.45	kilograms	4 oz		= 115 g
	g	grams	0.035	ounces	8 oz		= 225 g
	kg	kilograms	2.2	pounds	16 oz	= 1 lb	= 450 g
					32 oz	= 2 lb	= 900 g
					36 oz	= 2 1/4 lb	= 1,000 g (1 kg)
Volume	tsp	teaspoons	5.0	milliliters	1/4 tsp	= 1/24 oz	= 1 ml
	tbsp	tablespoons	15.0	milliliters	1/2 tsp	= 1/12 oz	= 2 ml
	fl oz	fluid ounces	29.57	milliliters	1 tsp	= 1/6 oz	= 5 ml
	c	cups	0.24	liters	1 tbsp	= 1/2 oz	= 15 ml
	pt	pints	0.47	liters	1 c	= 8 oz	= 250 ml
	qt	quarts	0.95	liters	2 c (1 pt)	= 16 oz	= 500 ml
	gal	gallons	3.785	liters	4 c (1 qt)	= 32 oz	= 1 l.
	ml	milliliters	0.034	fluid ounces	4 qt (1 gal)	= 128 oz	= 3 3/4 l.
Length	in.	inches	2.54	centimeters	3/8 in.	= 1 cm	
	ft	feet	30.48	centimeters	1 in.	= 2.5 cm	
	yd	yards	0.9144	meters	2 in.	= 5 cm	
	mi	miles	1.609	kilometers	2 1/2 in.	= 6.5 cm	
	km	kilometers	0.621	miles	12 in. (1 ft)	= 30 cm	
	m	meters	1.094	yards	1 yd	= 90 cm	
	cm	centimeters	0.39	inches	100 ft	= 30 m	
					1 mi	= 1.6 km	
Temperature	° F	Fahrenheit	5/9 (after subtracting 32)	Celsius	32° F	= 0° C	
					68 °F	= 20° C	
	° C	Celsius	9/5 (then add 32)	Fahrenheit	212° F	= 100° C	
Area	in.^{2}	square inches	6.452	square centimeters	1 in.^{2}	= 6.5 cm^2	
	ft^2	square feet	929.0	square centimeters	1 ft^2	= 930 cm^2	
	yd^2	square yards	8,361.0	square centimeters	1 yd^2	= 8,360 cm^2	
	a	acres	0.4047	hectares	1 a	= 4,050 m^2	